Cheesecakes

Simple and easy to make

NEW HOLLAND

Cheesecakes

Simple and easy to make

NEW HOLLAND

Contents

Introduction

We have assembled Old World recipes, New World recipes and an exotic mix of tropical and Eastern recipes for you to try. This is not a slimming cookbook, that's for sure, but remember that everything in moderation leads to a happy as well as a healthy existence. So while you should not be reaching for this cookbook on a daily basis, there is nothing wrong with the occasional tasty indulgence, particularly when they are as tasty and indulgent as the recipes on offer here!

We have included elegant single-serve recipes among the larger classic cheesecakes—this makes it easier to divide or multiply these recipes to make as many or as few as you like. Individual cheesecakes make for a great visual display if you are having a dinner party, and they also pack and travel well for picnics and lunches.

For the more traditional at heart, you will find wonderful well-known American and Continental treats along with exotic and perfumed offerings from further afield.

Among the many recipes you will encounter cheesecake flavours you may not be familiar with. And if you do not live in an area where Turkish, Lebanese or Middle Eastern foods are readily available, kashta cheese can be substituted with ricotta. However, it is well worth asking around as you may be surprised by what is available beyond your regular supermarket, and you will definitely enjoy and benefit from such a culinary excursion. For some of the more tropical cheesecakes try your local Chinatown or Asian grocery stores and be guided by what looks good and is in season. Remember—fresh is always best.

Baked or chilled, cheesecakes are one of the simplest of desserts and one of the most enjoyed.

Types of Cheese

Cheesecakes are usually made from fresh, unripened cheese varieties. The three most popular cheeses used in cheesecakes are:

Cream cheese
A mixture of milk and cream, which has a mild flavour and very smooth texture.

Cottage cheese
Which has a slightly acidic flavour and a grainy, paste-like texture.

Ricotta cheese
Which has a fine, moist texture and a sweet eggy flavour.

Types of Bases

Cheesecake is served with an edible base which can be made from a variety of different ingredients. The most common bases include:

Biscuit bases
Which are a combination of crushed sweet biscuits and butter, yet may use flavoured biscuits or have spices, coconut, nuts or other ingredients added.

Pastry bases
Which use sweet shortcrust pastry or shortbread pastry, and may be pre-baked.

Cereal bases
Using crushed cornflakes or similar, combined with butter, honey or melted marshmallow.

Sponge bases
Which may use a whole sponge, sponge fingers, or slices of Swiss roll.

A-Z Guide to Successful Cheesecakes

❊ Aluminium foil can be used to shield your microwave cheesecake by placing a 1 cm (¼ in) ring around the edge of the pan.

❊ Breakfast cereal can be crushed and combined with butter, honey or melted marshmallow for an interesting crust.

❊ Cream the cheese, egg yolks and sugar thoroughly before adding other ingredients to give a really smooth texture.

❊ Do not beat the egg whites into the mixture, fold them through.

❊ Elaborately decorated cheesecakes are best frozen without their decoration, then add the topping just prior to serving.

❊ Fold egg whites lightly but thoroughly into cheese mixture to avoid bubbles of egg white being left.

❊ Generously butter pans, unless they have a non-stick finish.

❊ Heat a knife and run it around the edge of the cheesecake pan to loosen a particularly stubborn cheesecake.

❊ Invert the base of springform pans before placing in the tin to avoid cheesecake becoming stuck on the ridge of the base.

❊ Jelly crystals combined with fruit juice make a quick and tasty glaze for your cheesecake.

❊ Keep cheesecakes covered in the refrigerator and they will last for 4–5 days.

❊ Loosen the sides of your unbaked cheesecake from the pan by running a hot damp cloth around the outside of the pan.

* Make a different base using sponge cake or slices of Swiss roll.

* Nasturtiums, roses, violets and other edible flowers can be used as an alternative to decorate your cheesecake.

* Open-freeze a cheesecake on its base, then wrap with freezer wrap or place into a large freezer bag.

* Pastry bases of sweet shortcrust or shortbread pastry are great for cheesecakes, but require slightly higher initial baking temperatures.

* Quark may be used as a low-fat alternative to cottage or cream cheese.

* Ricotta cheese is used mostly in Italian-style cheesecakes and is made from the whey, rather than the milk curd as in other cheesecakes.

* Soften cream cheese in the microwave on medium-high (70%) for easy beating.

* Thaw frozen cheesecakes in the refrigerator for 4–6 hours.

* Use a warm oven to completely dry washed cake pans to avoid rusting.

* Varieties of biscuits such as shortbreads will require less butter to bind them when crushed and used as a base.

* When pressing in crumb crust, use a straight-sided flat-based glass to make it easier.

* Extra flavour can be given to crumb crusts by mixing in a teaspoon of cinnamon, nutmeg or ginger powder.

* Yoghurt can substitute for cream in unbaked cheesecakes giving a tangy, acid flavour.

* Zealous cooks will amaze and delight with delicious cheesecakes.

Classic

Banana Cheesecake

SERVES 12

BASE

120g (4oz) digestive biscuits, finely crushed

⅓ cup linseed meal

60g (2oz) butter, melted

FILLING

500g (17oz) cream cheese

2 medium bananas, mashed

2 cups sour cream

1 cup sugar

3 eggs

1 tablespoon cornflour (cornstarch)

3 tablespoons lemon juice

1½ teaspoons vanilla

Preheat oven to 180°C (350°F).

BASE

Thoroughly mix biscuit crumbs, linseed meal and butter. Spread onto bottom of a lined 23cm (9in) springform tin. Cook for 10 minutes.

FILLING

Beat the cream cheese until soft and smooth, add the banana, sour cream and sugar and beat until smooth. Add the eggs one at a time, mixing thoroughly after each addition. Add the cornflour, lemon juice and vanilla. Mix thoroughly, pour into base. Bake for 1 hour. Turn off the oven and leave cheesecake in for another hour.

Top with whipped cream and roasted hazelnuts to serve.

Classic

Creamy Chocolate Cheesecake

SERVES 8

BASE

100g (3½oz) low-fat digestive biscuits

55g (2oz) butter

1 tablespoon golden syrup

FILLING

200g (7oz) cream cheese

2 tablespoons caster (superfine) sugar

100g (3½oz) semisweet chocolate drops

30g (1oz) cocoa powder, sifted

1 cup thickened cream

30g (1oz) semisweet chocolate, shaved

Preheat the oven to 180°C (350°F).

BASE
Put the biscuits into a plastic bag and crush with a rolling pin. Gently heat the butter and golden syrup until melted, stirring. Mix in the biscuits, then pack into an 18cm (7in) loose-bottomed cake tin and cook for 15 minutes or until crisp. Cool for 20 minutes.

FILLING
Beat the cream cheese with the sugar until soft. Melt half the chocolate drops in a bowl set over a saucepan of simmering water. Blend the cocoa to a paste with 2 tablespoons of boiling water. Stir into the melted chocolate and then fold in the cream cheese mixture. Stir in the remaining chocolate drops.

Whip half of the cream until it forms soft peaks. Fold it into the chocolate mixture, then spoon over the biscuit base. Refrigerate for 2 hours or until set. Remove from the tin. Whip the remaining cream and spread over the cheesecake and top with the chocolate shavings.

NOTE
To make this cheesecake even more decadent, beat a little fruity liqueur into the cream.

Honey Cheesecake

SERVES 10

BASE

½ cup chopped hazelnuts

90g (3oz) unsalted butter, melted

1½ cups digestive biscuit crumbs

¼ cup honey

FILLING

1kg (2lb 4oz) cream cheese,
*   softened*

1 cup honey

½ cup Cointreau

2 cups double cream, whipped

Preheat oven to 180°C (350°F).

BASE

Place hazelnuts on a baking tray and bake for 5 minutes, until lightly toasted. Remove and let cool, then mix with butter, biscuit crumbs and the honey.

Press mixture into the bottom of a 25cm (10in) springform tin. Set aside.

FILLING

With an electric mixer, beat together the cream cheese, honey and Cointreau, then fold in the whipped cream.

Spread filling evenly over the biscuit crust and chill for a few hours until firm.

Serve garnished with orange, lemon and lime zest curls.

Classic

Classic Unbaked Cheesecake

SERVES 8

BASE

*125g (4oz) plain sweet biscuits,
  crushed*

50g (1¾oz) butter, melted

FILLING

*500g (17oz) cottage cheese or
  cream cheese*

½ cup caster (superfine) sugar

2 tablespoons lemon juice

¼ cup milk

1 cup thickened cream

1 tablespoon gelatine

2 egg whites

BASE

Combine biscuits and butter together and press onto the base of a 22cm (8½in) springform tin. Refrigerate while preparing filling.

FILLING

Cream together the cheese and sugar until smooth. Beat in lemon juice and milk, then gently fold in cream.

Sprinkle the gelatine onto 2 tablespoons hot water and stir briskly until dissolved to a clear golden liquid. Add to cheese mixture.

Whip egg whites until stiff peaks form. Fold into cheese mixture. Pour into prepared tin. Refrigerate until firm.

Decorate with whipped cream and thin lemon twists.

Cheesecakes

Chocolate Fudge Cheesecake

SERVES 16

BASE

200g (7oz) plain sweet biscuits,
  crushed

100g (3½oz) butter, melted

FILLING

500g (17oz) cream cheese, softened

¾ cup caster (superfine) sugar

3 eggs

1 cup thickened cream

200g (7oz) dark chocolate, melted

2 x 50g (1¾oz) cherry chocolate
  bars, roughly chopped

Preheat oven to 140°C (285°F).

BASE

Combine biscuits and butter together, and press into the base of a lightly buttered 22cm (8½in) springform tin.

FILLING

Beat together the cheese and caster sugar until smooth.

Add the eggs and beat well. Fold through the cream, chocolate and chopped chocolate bars. Pour onto the prepared crumb base and bake for 1 hour and 45 minutes.

Turn off oven and allow cheesecake to cool in the oven. When cold, remove from tin and chill. Serve with whipped cream if desired.

Hazelnut Raspberry Cheesecake

SERVES 12

BASE

190g (6½oz) ameretti biscuits,
   finely crushed

60g (2oz) butter, melted

FILLING

1kg (2lb 4oz) cream cheese,
   softened

1¼ cups sugar

3 large eggs

1 cup sour cream

1 teaspoon vanilla essence

170g (6oz) hazelnut spread

⅓ cup raspberry conserve

Preheat oven to 165°C (330°F).

BASE

Combine crumbs and butter, press onto bottom of 23cm (9in) springform tin.

FILLING

Combine ¾ of the cream cheese and the sugar in an electric mixer and mix on medium speed until well blended. Add eggs one at a time, beating well after each addition. Blend in sour cream and vanilla, pour over base.

Combine remaining cream cheese and the hazelnut spread in the electric mixer, mix on medium speed until well blended. Add raspberry conserve, mix well.

Drop heaped tablespoonfuls of hazelnut mixture into plain cream cheese filling—do not swirl.

Bake for 1 hour and 25 minutes. Loosen cake from rim of tin, cool before removing. Serve with fresh raspberries.

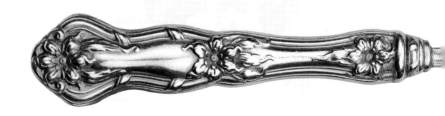

Banana Cream Cheesecake

SERVES 14

BASE

2 cups digestive biscuit crumbs

45g (1½oz) butter, melted

1 tablespoon sugar

FILLING

¾ cup sugar

600g (1lb 5oz) cream cheese, softened

4 eggs

1 cup puréed bananas (about 2 large)

2 teaspoons lemon juice

1 teaspoon vanilla extract

500g (17oz) strawberries

Preheat oven to 180°C (350°F).

BASE

Mix together the biscuit crumbs with the butter and sugar from the filling, then press mixture into a 20cm (8in) springform tin on sides and bottom.

FILLING

Beat together cream cheese and sugar until smooth and creamy. Add eggs, banana, lemon juice and vanilla. Mix well, scraping sides of bowl often. Pour into springform pan over the crumb crust.

Bake for about 1 hour or until firm in the centre. Allow to cool in pan. Remove outer ring of the springform tin and allow the cake to cool on a wire rack for about 1 hour.

Slice or halve strawberries and arrange in a circular pattern on top of cheesecake. Glaze with 1 tablespoon of jam if desired. Refrigerate for about 3 hours before serving.

Classic

Toffee Cheesecake

SERVES 12

BASE

100g (3½oz) vanilla wafers, finely
  crushed

90g (3oz) butter, melted

FILLING

400g (14oz) caramel sweets

1 cup semi-sweet chocolate chips

½ cup evaporated milk

3 chocolate bars covered in toffee,
  40g (1½oz) each

1kg (2lb 4oz) cream cheese

1½ cups sugar

2 tablespoons plain (all-purpose)
  flour, plus extra 2 teaspoons

4 whole eggs

2 egg yolks

⅓ cup double cream

Preheat oven to 175°C (345°F).

BASE

In a medium-size bowl combine wafer crumbs with the melted butter. Mix well. Press onto bottom and sides of a 23cm (9in) springform tin. Bake for 10 minutes, remove and allow to cool.

FILLING

Increase oven temperature to 200°C (400°F). In a saucepan over low heat, melt caramels together with the chocolate chips and evaporated milk, stir until smooth and pour into base. Break the chocolate bars into small pieces and sprinkle over the caramel layer.

Beat cream cheese until smooth. Add sugar and flour and beat until smooth. Add whole eggs and egg yolks one at a time, mixing well after each addition. Blend in cream, then pour over caramel and toffee layers. Wrap outside of pan with foil.

Set in a large pan that has been filled with 1.25cm (½in) of hot water. Bake for 15 minutes, reduce oven to 110°C (230°F) and bake for another hour. Remove from water, cool to room temperature then chill overnight in the refrigerator.

Top with whipped cream and chocolate caramel sweets to serve.

Cheesecakes

Frozen Peppermint Cheesecake

Serves 12

Base

300g (10½oz) mint slice biscuits

Filling

250g (9oz) cream cheese, softened

400g (14oz) condensed milk

1 cup hard peppermint sweets,
   crushed

2 cups thickened cream, whipped

Base

Place mint slices into a food processor and process until fine. Firmly press onto bottom of a 23cm (9in) springform tin. Chill.

Filling

Beat cream cheese at high speed with an electric mixer until fluffy. Add condensed milk and peppermint sweets. Beat well, then fold in whipped cream. Pour over base. Cover and freeze until firm.

Decorate with peppermint crisp bar and serve.

Classic

Almond Praline Cheesecake

Serves 12

Base

90g (3oz) digestive biscuits, finely
    crushed

½ cup slivered almonds, toasted
    and finely chopped

¼ cup brown sugar, firmly packed

50g (1¾oz) unsalted butter, melted

Filling

750g (1lb 10oz) cream cheese,
    softened

400g (14oz) canned condensed
    milk

3 eggs

1 teaspoon almond extract

Topping

⅓ cup dark brown sugar, firmly
    packed

⅓ cup thickened cream

½ cup slivered almonds, toasted
    and chopped

Preheat oven to 220°C (420°F).

Base

Combine crumbs, nuts, sugar and butter. Line a 23cm (9in) springform tin with baking paper and press crumb mixture onto the bottom.

Filling

In a large mixer bowl, beat cream cheese until fluffy. Gradually beat in condensed milk until smooth. Add eggs one at a time, mixing well after each addition, then add almond extract.

Pour into tin. Bake for 10 minutes, reduce heat to 150°C (300°F) and bake for a further 30 minutes.

Topping

Meanwhile, combine sugar and cream in a small saucepan. Cook and stir until sugar dissolves, then simmer 5 minutes or until thickened. Remove from heat, stir in almonds.

Top cheesecake with almond praline topping and chill before serving.

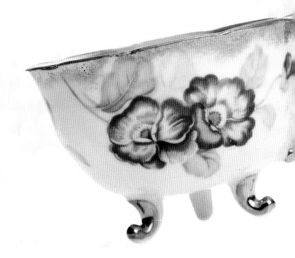

Cheesecakes

Poppyseed Cheesecake

SERVES 10

1 cup poppyseeds

500g (17oz) cream cheese

500g (17oz) ricotta

½ cup sugar

6 eggs

400ml (14fl oz) condensed milk

1 tablespoon vanilla extract

1 cup lemon curd (see below)

LEMON CURD

3 lemons, zest grated and juice
  strained

250g (9oz) sugar

75g (2½oz) butter

3 large eggs

Preheat the oven to 200°C (400°F).

Generously butter a 24cm non-stick cake tin.

Sprinkle half the poppyseeds over the base and sides of the cake tin, then tip out the excess and reserve the remaining poppyseeds.

Beat the cream cheese and ricotta until very smooth, then add the sugar and continue for 2 minutes. Add the eggs one at a time, beating well after each addition, then finally add the condensed milk and vanilla and beat for one more minute. Using a spatula, stir around the sides if necessary. Add the leftover poppyseeds and mix well to distribute them throughout the mixture.

Pour the mixture into the prepared tin and smooth the top gently by tapping the tin on the counter. Bake for 10 minutes, then reduce the heat to 160°C (320°F) and cook for a further 40 minutes, or until the mixture is still slightly wobbly. Allow the cake to cool in the tin, undisturbed until cold.

To make the lemon curd, place the lemon zest, juice, sugar and butter in the top of a double boiler or in a heatproof bowl over a saucepan of simmering water. Heat, stirring until the sugar dissolves and the mixture is quite warm. Do not allow to boil.

Add the eggs and mix with a whisk to distribute them thoroughly, and continue stirring while the mixture heats. Keep stirring until the mixture coats the back of a spoon, which indicates that the eggs have thickened and set.

When the cake is cold, carefully smooth the curd over the surface of the cake, and sprinkle the remaining poppyseeds over entire surface. When set, remove the side of the tin and serve.

Pecan Cheesecake

SERVES 12

BASE

180g (6oz) digestive biscuits, finely
  crushed

3 tablespoons sugar

50g (1¾oz) butter, melted

FILLING

1.25kg (2¾ lb) cream cheese,
  softened

1⅔ cups light brown sugar, firmly
  packed

40g (1½oz) butter, melted

5 eggs

1 teaspoon vanilla essence

1 cup pecans, chopped

Preheat oven to 165°C (330°F).

BASE

Combine biscuits, sugar and butter, mixing well. Press into bottom of 25cm (10in) springform tin, chill.

FILLING

   Beat cream cheese in an electric mixer until light and fluffy, gradually add brown sugar and butter, mixing well. Add eggs, one at a time, beating well after each addition. Stir in vanilla and pecans. Spoon filling into tin and bake for 1 hour.

   Turn oven off. Allow cheesecake to cool in oven for 30 minutes. Cool to room temperature then refrigerate for 8 hours. Remove sides of springform tin.

   Decorate with extra pecans and serve with whipped cream.

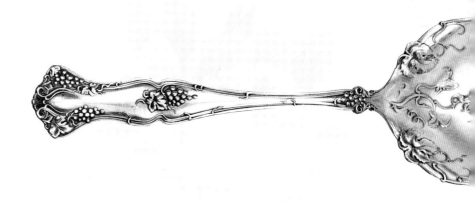

Lemon Sultana Cheesecake

SERVES 12

BASE

½ cup plain (all-purpose) flour

¼ cup cornflour (cornstarch)

¼ cup custard powder

1 tablespoon icing sugar

60g (2oz) butter

1 egg yolk

iced water

⅓ cup caster (superfine) sugar

1 tablespoon cinnamom

1 tablespoon cardamom

FILLING

375g (13oz) cream cheese, softened

¼ cup natural yoghurt

½ cup caster (superfine) sugar

2 eggs

1 teaspoon vanilla essence

zest of 1 lemon

170g (6oz) sultanas

TOPPING

½ cup double cream

2 teaspoons lemon juice

zest of ½ lemon

Preheat oven to 180°C (350°F).

BASE

Sift flour, cornflour, custard powder and icing sugar into a large mixing bowl. Rub in butter with your fingers until mixture resembles coarse breadcrumbs. Make a well in the centre of the mixture and stir in egg yolk and enough water to make a firm dough. Wrap in cling wrap and refrigerate for 30 minutes.

Roll out pastry to fit the base of a greased 20cm (8in) springform tin. Using a fork, prick pastry base and bake for 10 minutes. Set aside to cool.

In a bowl mix together the sugar, cinnamon and cardamom. Spread evenly over cooled pastry base.

FILLING

Place cream cheese, yoghurt, sugar, eggs, vanilla essence and lemon zest in a mixing bowl and beat until smooth. Fold in sultanas.

Spoon mixture into prepared base. Reduce oven temperature to 180°C (350°F) and bake for 20–25 minutes or until firm. Turn off oven and leave cheesecake to cool in oven with door ajar.

TOPPING

Place cream, lemon juice and zest in a small saucepan and bring to a boil, then simmer, stirring, for 5 minutes or until mixture thickens. Pour topping over cooled cheesecake and chill until required.

Amaretto Cheesecake

SERVES 12
½ cup whole almonds
500g (17oz) cream cheese
¾ cup sugar
3 eggs
1 teaspoon vanilla essence
2 tablespoons Amaretto
¾ cup sour cream

Preheat oven to 170°C (335°F).

Spread nuts in a baking pan and bake for 8 minutes or until lightly toasted. Cool and finely chop.

With an electric mixer, beat cheese and sugar until smooth. Mix in eggs, vanilla, Amaretto and sour cream, then stir in nuts.

Pour cream cheese mixture into a greased 23cm (9in) springform tin. Bake in the middle of the oven for 25 minutes or until just barely set.

Turn off the oven, leave the door ajar, and allow to cool in the oven for 1 hour longer. Chill.

To serve, remove tin sides and cut into wedges. Decorate with toasted flaked almonds.

Cheesecakes

Cheesecake with Strawberries

SERVES 12

BASE

175g (6oz) butter

350g (12oz) biscuit crumbs

FILLING

60g (2oz) brown sugar

250g (9oz) cream cheese, softened

3 eggs, lightly beaten

1 cup sugar

1 teaspoon lemon juice

2 teaspoons vanilla extract

2 cups sour cream

½ cup fresh strawberries

Preheat oven to 160°C (320°F).

BASE

Melt butter in saucepan over medium heat. Stir in crumbs and sugar.

Take a 25cm (10in) springform tin and pack the mixture into sides and bottom to make a base. Bake for 10 minutes.

FILLING

Beat cream cheese, eggs, sugar, lemon juice and vanilla together well, then mix in sour cream. Pour over crust, raise oven temperature to 180°C (350°F) and bake for 1 hour. Let stand at least 2 hours. Chill until required. Use fresh strawberries to top the cheesecake.

Classic

Ricotta Cheesecake

SERVES 12

BASE

180g (6oz) digestive biscuits, finely crushed

FILLING

1.3kg (3lb) ricotta cheese, drained

2 cups sugar

8 egg yolks

½ cup plain (all-purpose) flour, sifted

zest of 1 lemon

1 teaspoon vanilla essence

8 egg whites

½ cup thickened cream, whipped

Preheat oven to 220°C (420°F).

BASE

Sprinkle a 30cm (12in) springform tin with the biscuit crumbs.

FILLING

Beat ricotta until smooth, gradually add ¾ of the sugar, then add egg yolks one at a time, mixing well after each addition. Beat in flour, lemon zest and vanilla.

Beat egg whites with remaining sugar. Fold whipped cream and egg whites into ricotta mixture and turn into prepared tin. Bake for 10 minutes, lower temperature to 180°C (350°F) and bake for 1 hour. Turn off heat and allow to cool in oven with door closed. Dust with icing sugar before serving.

Cheesecakes

Chocolate Caramel Cheesecake

SERVES 12

BASE

150g (5oz) digestive biscuits, finely
crushed

50g (1¾oz) butter, melted

FILLING

¼ cup evaporated milk

380g (13oz) canned caramel

1 cup pecan nuts, chopped

500g (17oz) cream cheese

½ cup sugar

2 eggs

1 teaspoon vanilla essence

¾ cup chocolate chips, melted

Preheat oven to 180°C (350°F).

BASE

Combine the crumbs and melted butter. Press mixture
evenly into a 23cm (9in) springform tin. Bake for 8
minutes. Remove from oven and allow to cool.

FILLING

Combine milk and caramel in a heavy-based saucepan.
Cook over low heat until melted, stirring often. Pour over
biscuit base. Sprinkle pecans evenly over caramel layer and
set aside.

Beat cream cheese at high speed with electric mixer until
light and fluffy. Gradually add sugar, mixing well. Add
eggs one at a time, beating well after each addition. Stir
in vanilla and melted chocolate, beat until blended. Pour
over pecan layer.

Bake for 30 minutes. Remove from oven and run
knife around edge of tin to release sides. Cool to room
temperature. Cover and chill for 8 hours.

Decorate with a chopped flaky chocolate bar and
chopped jersey caramels. Serve with whipped cream.

White Chocolate Cheesecake with Raspberry Sauce

Serves 12

Filling

1 cup white chocolate chips

500g (17oz) cream cheese, softened

¾ cup sugar

3 eggs

1½ teaspoons vanilla essence

¾ cup sour cream

Raspberry sauce

½ cup sugar

½ cup water

2½ cups raspberries

½ cup thickened cream, whipped

Preheat oven to 165°C (330°F).

Filling

Place chocolate in a double boiler and heat over hot water until it melts. Stir to blend, then cool to room temperature.

With an electric mixer, blend cream cheese and sugar until smooth. Mix in eggs, vanilla and sour cream. Stir in melted chocolate—it is important to have the cheesecake ingredients and the melted chocolate close to the same temperature when they are combined so that they blend together smoothly.

Pour into a greased 23cm (9in) springform tin. Bake in the middle of the oven for 25 minutes or until just barely set. Turn off the oven, leave the door ajar, and allow to cool in oven for 1 hour longer. Chill.

Raspberry Sauce

Place sugar and water in a saucepan, bring to the boil and simmer for 5 minutes. Meanwhile, purée 2 cups of the raspberries in a blender. Add the puréed raspberries to the sugar syrup, simmer for another 3 minutes. Remove from heat and cool.

Pipe cream onto the cheesecake and top with the remaining raspberries. Serve with the raspberry sauce.

Cappuccino Cheesecake

SERVES 12

BASE

1½ cups finely chopped nuts
(almonds, walnuts)

2 tablespoons sugar

50g (1¾oz) butter, melted

FILLING

1kg (2lb 4oz) cream cheese,
softened

1 cup sugar

3 tablespoons plain (all-purpose)
flour

4 large eggs

1 cup sour cream

1 tablespoon instant coffee granules

¼ teaspoon cinnamon powder

¼ cup boiling water

Preheat oven to 160°C (320°F).

BASE

Combine nuts, sugar and butter, press onto bottom of
23cm (9in) springform tin. Bake for 10 minutes, remove
from oven and allow to cool. Increase oven temperature to
230°C (450°F).

FILLING

Combine cream cheese, sugar and flour in an electric
mixer, mix on medium speed until well blended. Add eggs,
one at a time, mixing well after each addition. Blend in
sour cream.

Dissolve coffee granules and cinnamon in water. Cool,
then gradually add to cream cheese mixture, mixing until
well blended. Pour over base.

Bake for 10 minutes. Reduce oven temperature to
120°C (250°F) and continue baking for 1 hour.

Loosen cake from rim, allow to cool before removing.
Chill. Serve topped with whipped cream and coffee beans.

Classic

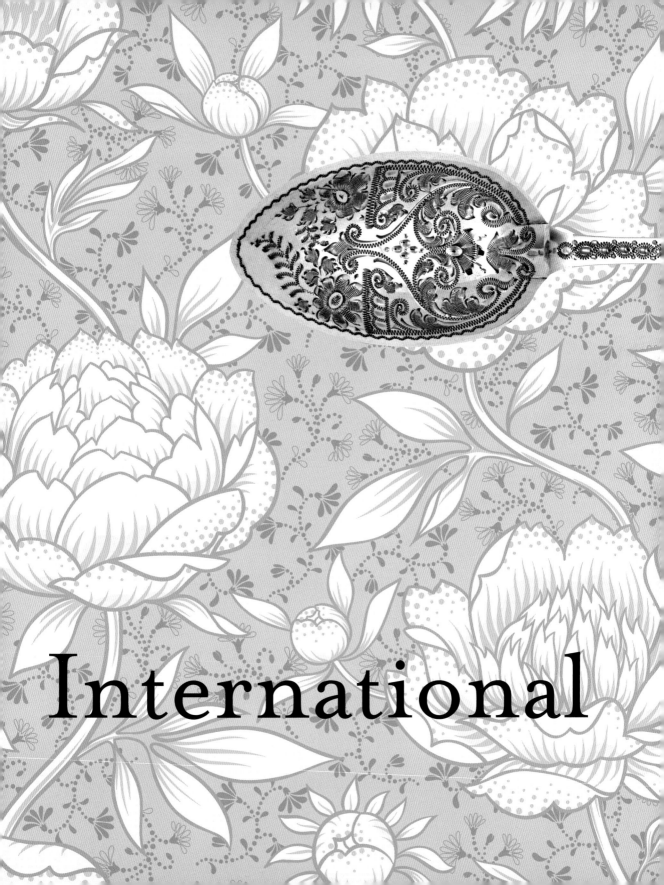

International

Russian Cheesecake

Serves 12

Base

3 tablespoons sugar

3 tablespoons brown sugar

½ teaspoon nutmeg

50g (1¾oz) butter, softened

¾ cup ground walnuts

¾ cup plain (all-purpose) flour

1 teaspoon baking powder

Filling

700g (1lb 9oz) cream cheese,
  softened

200g (7oz) soft ricotta

1½ cups sugar

6 large eggs, separated

juice and zest of 1 large lemon

3 tablespoons plain
  (all-purpose) flour

1 cup thickened cream

Preheat the oven to 200°C (400°F).

Base

Butter a 28cm (11in) non-stick springform cake tin.
Remove the base of the cake tin from the sides and lay a
piece of baking paper over the base. Replace the sides to
hold the paper in place.

Using a food processor, pulse together all the base
ingredients until a stiff dough forms. Roll out the dough
and press over the base of the cake tin. Bake for 10 minutes
then remove from the oven and cool.

Filling

Combine the cream cheese, ricotta and 1 cup of sugar and
beat for 3 minutes or until the mixture is smooth. Add the
egg yolks one at a time, beating well after each addition.
Add the juice and zest of the lemon and the plain flour,
and mix until combined.

In a separate bowl, beat the egg whites until foaming,
then add the remaining half cup of sugar, sprinkling the
sugar into the egg whites while the motor is running. When
all the sugar has been added, raise the speed of the mixer
to the fastest, then allow the egg whites to beat until they
are thick and glossy.

In a separate bowl, whip the cream until soft peaks form.
Fold the cream and the egg whites into the cheese mixture
and combine thoroughly. Pour into the cooled crust.

Bake for 10 minutes, then reduce the heat to 150°C
(300°F) and cook for an hour. Turn off the heat and
leave the cake in the oven undisturbed. When the cake has
cooled, remove from the oven and chill overnight.

Sprinkle with icing sugar and serve.

Kashta Cheesecake

SERVES 12

BASE

1 cup semolina

2 tablespoons icing sugar

zest of 1 lemon

1 teaspoon cinnamon

¼ teaspoon nutmeg

100g (3½oz) butter, chopped

⅔ cup water

FILLING

650g (1lb 6oz) cream cheese,
    softened

250g (9oz) kashta cheese

1½ cups sugar

6 large eggs, separated

juice and zest of 1 large lemon

¾ cup walnuts, ground

50g (1¾oz) butter, softened

¾ cup plain (all-purpose) flour

1 cup thickened cream

1 cup sultanas

Preheat oven to 200°C (400°F).

BASE

Line a 23 cm (9in) springform tin with baking paper.
Mix semolina, sugar, zest and spices together, rub in
butter until mixture resembles fine breadcrumbs. Add
enough water to make ingredients come together.

Press evenly onto the bottom of the tin, line with baking
paper, half-fill with dried beans and blind bake for 10
minutes. Remove the paper and beans.

FILLING

Meanwhile, combine the cream cheese, kashta and 1 cup
of sugar in an electric mixer and beat for 4 minutes until
smooth. Add the egg yolks one at a time, beating well after
each addition. Add the lemon juice and zest, walnuts,
butter and flour and mix until combined.

In a separate bowl, beat the egg whites until foaming
then add the remaining sugar. Beat until thick and glossy.

In another bowl, beat the cream until soft peaks form.
Fold the cream and egg whites into the cheese mixture,
combine thoroughly. Pour into the cooled base and
sprinkle over the sultanas.

Bake for 10 minutes then reduce heat to 150°C (300°F)
and cook for an hour. Turn off the oven and leave the cake
in the oven. When cake has cooled, remove and refrigerate
overnight.

Dust with icing sugar to serve.

NOTE

Kashta is a heavy cream style of fresh cheese. Ask for it in
local Lebanese and Middle Eastern supermarkets.

Cheesecake Sedap

Serves 12

Base

200g (7oz) shortbread biscuits

25g (¾oz) shredded coconut

Filling

500g (17oz) cream cheese

250g (9oz) ricotta cheese

1 cup sugar

1 vanilla bean, split lengthwise

4 large eggs

¼ cup very strong black tea

½ cup shredded coconut, lightly toasted

10–12 fresh lychees

Preheat oven to 160°C (320°F).

Base

Finely grind biscuits in a food processor. Mix together with the coconut, press onto bottom of a lined 23cm (9in) springform tin.

Bake until crisp, about 10 minutes. Cool on rack while preparing filling.

Filling

Using an electric mixer, beat together cream cheese, ricotta and sugar until smooth. Scrape in seeds from vanilla bean, then beat in eggs one at a time until just blended. Beat in the tea, then pour filling over base.

Bake until filling is just set and puffed around edges, about 45 minutes.

Cool, then release tin sides. Sprinkle toasted coconut around top edge of cake. Top with fresh lychees and serve.

New York-Style Cheesecake

SERVES 12

BASE

120g (4oz) digestive biscuits, finely
crushed

¾ cup sugar

50g (1¾ oz) butter, melted

FILLING

1½ cups sour cream

1 cup sugar

2 eggs

1 teaspoon vanilla essence

500g (17oz) cream cheese, broken
into small pieces

40g (1½ oz) butter, melted

Preheat oven to 165°C (330°F).

BASE

Blend the biscuit crumbs, sugar and melted butter, then
line the bottom of an ungreased 23cm (9in) springform
tin.

FILLING

Blend the sour cream, sugar, eggs and vanilla in a food
processor for 1 minute. Add the cream cheese, blend until
smooth. While blending, pour the melted butter through
the top of the machine. Pour cream cheese mixture into
the springform tin.

Bake in the lower third of the oven for 45 minutes,
remove from oven and cool.

Refrigerate for 4 hours, preferably overnight. Dust with
plenty of icing sugar before cutting and serving. Serve with
whipped cream.

International

Black Forest Cheesecake

Serves 10

Base

1½ cups digestive biscuit crumbs

60g (2oz) butter, melted

¼ cup cocoa powder

¼ cup sugar

Filling

750g (1lb 10oz) cream cheese

1½ cups sugar

4 eggs

¼ cup amaretto

¼ cup maraschino cherry juice

125g (4oz) semi-sweet chocolate, melted

½ cup sour cream

Preheat oven to 180°C (350°F).

Base

Combine the biscuit crumbs, butter, cocoa and the sugar and mix well. Firmly press into the bottom and 2.5cm (1in) up the sides of a 22cm (8½in) springform tin. Set aside.

Filling

Beat cream cheese until fluffy with an electric mixer, gradually add sugar and mix well.

Add eggs one at a time, beating well after each addition, then add the amaretto and cherry juice until well blended.

Pour into crust and bake for 1 hour.

When cooked, remove from oven and allow to cool for 2–3 hours on a wire rack.

While cake is cooling, combine melted chocolate and sour cream, and when cake is cool, spread evenly over top of cheesecake.

Chill in refrigerator overnight. Before serving, garnish with whipped cream and maraschino cherries.

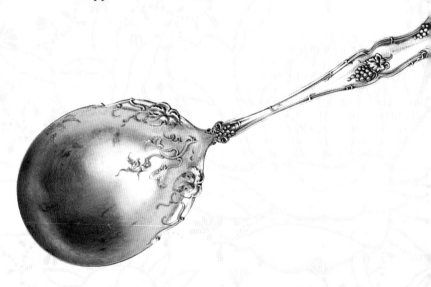

Cheesecakes

Italian Cheesecake

66 *SERVES 12*

BASE

150g (5oz) digestive biscuits, finely
  crushed

50g (1¾oz) butter, melted

FILLING

750g (1lb 10oz) ricotta cheese

250g (9oz) cream cheese

½ cup sugar

2 tablespoons brandy

2 tablespoons vanilla essence

3 large egg yolks

Preheat oven to 175°C (345°F).

BASE

Mix together the biscuit crumbs and butter and press into
a 23cm (9in) springform tin lined with baking paper.

FILLING

In a large mixing bowl, beat together the ricotta and cream
cheese until smooth.

   Add sugar, brandy and vanilla, mix well. Add the egg
yolks and beat until well blended. Pour into base.

   Bake for 30 minutes, or until the centre is set.

International

Jamaican Rice Cheesecake

SERVES 12

BASE

60g (2oz) digestive biscuits, finely
    crushed

1 cup finely chopped almonds

¼ cup sugar

50g (1¾oz) butter, melted

FILLING

2 cups cooked rice

1½ cups sour cream

90g (3oz) butter, melted

500g (17oz) ricotta cheese

500g (17oz) cream cheese, softened

1½ cups sugar

4 large eggs

¼ cup rum

1 teaspoon vanilla essence

TOPPING

¾ cup sour cream

2 tablespoons sugar

½ teaspoon vanilla essence

Preheat oven to 180°C (350°F).

BASE

Combine biscuit crumbs, almonds, sugar and butter in
a medium mixing bowl. Press into bottom and 25mm up
sides of an ungreased 23cm (9in) springform tin.

FILLING

Combine rice, sour cream and butter in food processor or
blender, process until well blended and set aside.

Beat ricotta, cream cheese and sugar in a large mixing
bowl until light and fluffy. Add eggs one at a time, beating
well after each addition. Blend in rum, vanilla and rice
mixture.

Pour filling into prepared base. Bake for 1 hour. Turn
oven off and leave cheesecake in oven an additional 2
hours. Cool. Refrigerate at least 8 hours or overnight.

TOPPING

Combine sour cream, sugar and vanilla, spread over
cheesecake. Decorate with fresh tropical fruit and shredded
coconut.

Ginger Honey Cheesecake

SERVES 12

BASE

250g (9oz) gingernut biscuits,
*   finely crushed*

1 tablespoon sugar

50g (1³⁄₄oz) butter, chilled

FILLING

500g (17oz) cream cheese, softened

¹⁄₂ cup honey

¹⁄₂ cup sugar

2 large eggs, at room temperature

300g (10¹⁄₂oz) kashta cheese

1 tablespoon lemon juice

1¹⁄₂ teaspoons vanilla essence

³⁄₄ cup dates, finely minced

2 tablespoons glacé ginger, finely
*   minced*

Preheat oven to 180°C (350°F).

BASE

Butter only the sides of a 23cm (9in) springform tin. Mix the crumbs and sugar in a bowl. Add the butter and rub it in well with your fingers. Distribute the crumbs loosely but evenly in the pan and push them slightly up the sides. Cover and chill while you make the filling.

FILLING

Using an electric mixer, cream the cream cheese, honey and sugar until light and fluffy. Beat in the eggs one at a time, then add the remaining ingredients and continue to beat until evenly blended. Pour the filling into the tin and bake for 1 hour and 15 minutes. Cool thoroughly on a rack, then cover, still in the tin, and refrigerate for 12 hours before removing from the tin and slicing.

Dust the cheesecake with icing sugar before serving.

NOTE

Kashta is a heavy cream style of fresh cheese. Ask for it in local Lebanese and Middle Eastern supermarkets.

Turkish Delight Cheesecake

SERVES 4

BASE

¾ cup ground almonds

20g (⅔oz) butter, melted

FILLING

1½ tablespoons gelatine

¼ cup water

450g (15oz) cream cheese

¾ cup milk

¾ cup sugar

2 tablespoons rose water

16 pieces Turkish delight

BASE

Stir together almonds and butter in a small bowl.

Line four 10cm (4in) springform tins with baking paper, then press mixture evenly onto bottoms of tins.

FILLING

Soften gelatine in water in small saucepan, stir over low heat until dissolved. Beat cream cheese, milk, sugar and rose water with an electric mixer until well blended.

Divide filling evenly between each base, place in the refrigerator for 3 hours or overnight.

Decorate with Turkish delight and serve.

Yoghurt Cheesecake

SERVES 12

BASE

180g (6oz) digestive biscuits, finely
   crushed

1 teaspoon cinnamon

½ teaspoon ground cardamom

2 tablespoons sugar

90g (3oz) butter, melted

FILLING

2 tablespoons gelatine

¼ cup warm water

250g (9oz) kashta cheese

250g (9oz) cottage cheese

1 cup yoghurt

3 eggs, separated

1¼ cups sugar

pinch of salt

zest of 1 large lemon

2 tablespoons lemon juice

1 cup thickened cream

50g (1¾oz) Persian fairy floss

BASE

Mix together the biscuits crumbs, cinnamom, cardamom, sugar and butter. Firmly press onto the bottom of a 23cm (9in) springform tin. Chill until ready to use.

FILLING

Dissolve the gelatine in the water.

Beat together the kashta, cottage cheese and yoghurt. Set aside.

In a double boiler, beat the egg yolks with ¾ cup of the sugar, the salt and lemon zest. Put over simmering water and cook, stirring constantly for 5 minutes.

Add the gelatine and stir until well combined. Remove from heat and cool slightly.

Stir in the cheese mixture and the lemon juice.

Beat the egg whites until they form soft peaks, add the remaining sugar, and continue beating until stiff. Fold into the cheese mixture. Whip the cream and fold in.

Pour the filling into the prepared base and chill for 8 hours or overnight.

Decorate with Persian fairy floss and serve.

NOTE

Kashta is a heavy cream style of fresh cheese. Ask for it in local Lebanese and Middle Eastern supermarkets.

German Cheesecake

SERVES 12

BASE

2 cups plain (all-purpose) flour

½ cup sugar

1 teaspoon baking powder

60g (2oz) butter

1 large egg

FILLING

750g (1lb 10oz) cottage cheese

½ cup cornflour (cornstarch)

1 teaspoon baking powder

1 cup sugar

4 large eggs

zest of ½ small lemon

½ teaspoon vanilla essence

1 cup sour cream

1 cup raisins

Preheat oven to 190°C (375°F).

BASE

In a large mixing bowl, blend together flour, sugar and baking powder. Cut in butter. Add egg and knead until well mixed. Divide the dough in half and use one half to line the bottom of a greased 23cm (9in) springform tin, the other half to line the sides. Chill.

FILLING

Press cottage cheese through a sieve. Combine cornflour and baking powder, set aside. In a large mixing bowl, combine the cottage cheese, sugar, eggs, lemon zest and vanilla. Beat until smooth. Add the cornflour mixture and blend well. Stir in sour cream and raisins. Pour the filling into the prepared base.

Bake for 1 hour, or until done—the centre will remain soft. Turn off the oven and, with the door ajar, allow the cake to cool to room temperature.

Bedouin Date Cheesecake

SERVES 12

BASE

20g (²⁄₃oz) butter

1 cup self-raising flour

¼ cup rolled oats

½ teaspoon ground ginger

4-5 tablespoons water

FILLING

225g (8oz) dates

½ cup unsweetened orange juice

1kg (2lb 4oz) ricotta cheese

4 eggs, lightly beaten

1¼ cups condensed milk

½ cup raisins, chopped

zest of 1 large lemon

2 tablespoons sugar

100g (3½oz) kataifi pastry

Preheat oven to 200°C (400°F).

BASE

In a bowl, rub butter into the flour until crumbly. Mix in oats, ginger and enough of the water to make a stiff, dry dough.

Roll out dough to a circle 1cm (¼in) thick. Carefully press into the base of a 25cm (10in) springform tin. Line with baking paper, half-fill with dried beans and blind bake for 10 minutes, remove the paper and beans. Set aside and allow to cool.

FILLING

Meanwhile, add dates and orange juice to a small saucepan, simmer gently until reduced to a soft paste. Cool.

Spread evenly over the base. Chill until ready to serve.

Beat together the cheese and eggs, then gradually beat in condensed milk until smooth.

Stir in raisins, lemon zest and sugar. Pour the mixture into base and top evenly with kataifi.

Bake for 15 minutes. Reduce heat to 190°C (375°F) and continue baking for 1½ hours or until a skewer inserted in the centre comes out clean. Cool on a wire rack.

International

Yoghurt, Rose and Date Cheesecake

SERVES 12

BASE

200g (7oz) digestive biscuits

75g (2½oz) butter, melted

FILLING

½ cup caster (superfine) sugar

¼ cup fresh orange juice, strained

2 tablespoons water

1½ tablespoons gelatine

1¼ cups thickened cream

500g (17oz) Greek yoghurt

3 teaspoons rose water

4 large fresh dates, sliced

1 tablespoon honey

BASE

Line the base and sides of a 23cm (9in) springform tin with baking paper.

Place the biscuits in a food processor and process until finely crushed. Add the butter and process until combined. Transfer to the lined tin, press the mixture firmly over the base. Place in the refrigerator for 30 minutes.

FILLING

Meanwhile, place the caster sugar and orange juice in a saucepan over low heat. Stir until the sugar dissolves.

Combine the water and gelatine in a small saucepan, stir over low heat until dissolved. Add the gelatine mixture to the orange juice mixture.

Beat the cream until soft peaks form.

Place the yoghurt in a large bowl, beat in the rose water, then the orange juice mixture. Use a metal spoon to fold in cream. Pour filling over the base. Top with slices of fresh date and drizzle with honey. Cover with a large plate and refrigerate overnight to set.

Cheesecakes

Fruit

Orange, Cardamom and Lime Cheesecake

SERVES 12

BASE

150g (5oz) plain sweet biscuits,
  finely crushed

90g (3oz) butter, melted

FILLING

200g (7oz) cream cheese, softened

½ teaspoon ground cardamom

2 tablespoons brown sugar

zest of 1 orange

zest of 2 limes

3 teaspoons orange juice

3 teaspoons lime juice

1 egg, lightly beaten

½ cup condensed milk

2 tablespoons thickened cream,
  whipped

Preheat oven to 180°C (350°F).

BASE

Combine biscuits and butter in a bowl and mix to
combine. Press biscuit mixture over base and sides of
a well-oiled 23cm (9in) springform tin. Bake for 5–8
minutes, then remove from oven and set aside to cool.

FILLING

Place cream cheese, cardamom, sugar, orange and lime
zest, and orange and lime juice in a mixing bowl and beat
until creamy. Beat in egg, then mix in condensed milk and
fold in cream.

Spoon mixture into prepared base and bake for 25–30
minutes or until just firm. Turn oven off and allow
cheesecake to cool in oven with door ajar. Chill before
serving.

Serve decorated with toasted coconut.

Fruit

Spiced Plum Cheesecake

SERVES 12

BASE

75g (2½oz) butter, melted

75g (2½oz) almond meal

75g (2½oz) sweet biscuits, finely
   crushed

FILLING

825g (1lb 13oz) canned plums in
   juice, drained

250g (9oz) kashta cheese

⅓ cup sour cream

⅔ cup caster (superfine) sugar

1 teaspoon vanilla essence

⅓ cup hot milk

¼ cup cornflour (cornstarch)

4 eggs, separated

Preheat oven to 210°C (410°F).

BASE

Combine the butter, almond meal and biscuits crumbs in a bowl and mix well. Press into the base of a 25cm (10in) springform tin.

FILLING

Arrange the plums, cut-side down, over the base.

Place the kashta, sour cream, ¼ cup of the caster sugar and the vanilla in an electric mixer and beat until smooth. Add the hot milk and beat until smooth, then add the cornflour and egg yolks and mix well.

In a clean bowl, whisk the egg whites to firm peaks, then whisk in the remaining sugar to make a firm meringue. Fold into the cheese mixture, then pour over the plum base.

Bake for 10 minutes, then reduce the temperature to 160°C (320°F) and bake for another 1 hour and 20 minutes or until a skewer inserted in the centre of the cake comes out clean.

Allow to cool, run a sharp knife around the inside of the tin and remove. Serve dusted with icing sugar.

NOTE

Kashta is a heavy cream style of fresh cheese. Ask for it in local Lebanese and Middle Eastern supermarkets.

Upside-down Orange Cheesecake

SERVES 12

BASE
65g ground almonds
⅓ cup caster (superfine) sugar
⅓ cup plain (all-purpose) flour
⅓ cup butter

FILLING
2 cups sugar
1 cup water
3 whole oranges, thinly sliced
500g (17oz) cream cheese, at room temperature
2 tablespoons Grand Marnier or Cointreau
1 tablespoon lemon juice
1 tablespoon gelatine
1¼ cups thickened cream, whipped
seeds of 1 pomegranate

Preheat oven to 160°C (320°F).

BASE
Place the almonds, sugar, flour and butter in a food processor, process until mixture forms a paste. Press into the base of a greased 20cm (8in) springform tin and bake for 20–25 minutes. Allow to cool, then turn out.

FILLING
Place the sugar and water together in a large saucepan and bring to the boil. Simmer, stirring until the sugar dissolves, add orange slices and simmer gently for 10–15 minutes. Remove the oranges carefully from the syrup and drain on absorbent paper. Reserve the syrup.

Arrange the best orange slices over the base and sides of the tin in an overlapping pattern (remember that the filling will only half-fill the tin). Chop enough of the remaining slices to fill ½ cup.

Place the cream cheese in a bowl and beat until smooth, gradually beat in the liqueur, lemon juice and chopped orange.

Whisk the gelatine into ½ a cup of the hot reserved orange syrup until dissolved, allow to cool. Add the gelatine mixture to the cheese mixture and beat until well mixed.

Lightly whip the cream and fold it gently into the cheese mixture. And the pomegranate seeds. Pour the mixture into the prepared tin. Place baked base on top and press down until level. Refrigerate for 3 hours.

Place the cheesecake upside down on a serving platter, then remove the mould. Brush top of cheesecake with remaining orange syrup before serving.

Durian Cheesecake

SERVES 8

BASE

150g (5oz) butter, melted

125g (4oz) chocolate cream-filled biscuits, finely crushed

125g (4oz) digestive biscuits, finely crushed

FILLING

1 tablespoon gelatine

2½ tablespoons warm water

250g (9oz) cream cheese

70g (2½oz) caster (superfine) sugar

250g (9oz) durian flesh

½ cup plain yoghurt

¾ cup thickened cream

BASE

Wrap the base of an 18 x 18cm (7 x 7in) cake tin with aluminium foil.

Slowly drizzle the melted butter into the biscuit crumbs, stirring until almost combined (you might not need to use all the butter). Press into cake tin and chill in refrigerator until firm, about 30 minutes.

FILLING

Add the gelatine to the water, dissolve and set aside.

Beat the cream cheese and sugar until creamy and light, then add the durian and continue to beat until well combined.

Pour in the gelatine mixture and yoghurt, stir until combined.

Add the cream and slowly stir until the mixture is creamy and well mixed.

Pour the filling into the tin and chill for at least 3 hours or overnight.

Cheesecakes

Coconut Mango Cheesecake

SERVES 12

BASE

180g (6oz) digestive biscuits, finely
   crushed

1½ cups desiccated coconut,
   toasted

¼ cup sugar

90g (3oz) butter, melted

FILLING

1kg (2lb 4oz) cream cheese,
   softened

¾ cup sugar

3 large whole eggs

1 large egg yolk

400ml (13½fl oz) coconut cream

1 cup thickened cream

1 cup desiccated coconut

MANGO PURÉE

½ fresh mango

Preheat oven to 165°C (330°F).

BASE

Wrap outside of 23cm (9in) springform tin with foil. Mix biscuit crumbs, coconut and sugar in a medium bowl. Add butter and mix. Press mixture onto bottom and up sides of prepared tin. Chill while preparing filling.

FILLING

Beat cream cheese and sugar in a large bowl until blended. Add whole eggs one at a time, beating after each addition. Beat in egg yolk. Add coconut cream, thickened cream and coconut, beat until just blended. Pour into base.

Bake until puffed and golden, about 1 hour and 25 minutes. Transfer to a rack, cool completely. Refrigerate until well chilled.

Using a small knife, cut around cheesecake to loosen. Remove tin sides.

MANGO PURÉE

Purée mango in blender until smooth. Transfer to a small bowl, sweeten with sugar if necessary. Serve cheesecake with mango purée.

Fruit

Summer Apricot Cheesecake

SERVES 10

BASE

1 cup sweet biscuit crumbs

60g (2oz) butter, melted

FILLING

1 tablespoon gelatine

500g (17oz) cream cheese, softened

400g (14oz) canned condensed
  milk

½ cup lemon juice

½ cup apricot purée

1 tablespoon Cointreau

400g (14oz) canned apricot halves

2 tablespoons toasted,
  flaked almonds

BASE

Combine biscuit crumbs and butter, press into base of a
20cm (8in) springform tin and chill.

FILLING

Heat gelatine with ¼ cup water until melted and clear.

Beat cream cheese until smooth, add gelatine mixture,
condensed milk, lemon juice, apricot purée and
Cointreau. Mix well until smooth. Pour into crumb base
and chill for 2–3 hours.

Top with apricot halves and press toasted almond flakes
onto sides before serving.

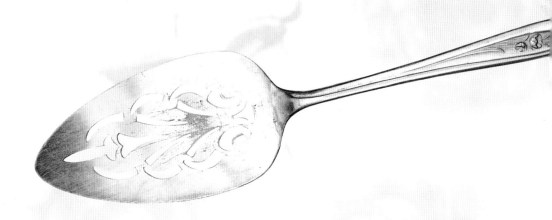

Blackberry Cheesecake

SERVES 12

BASE

150g (5oz) digestive biscuits, finely
  crushed

¼ cup sugar

1 tablespoon cinnamon

50g (1¾oz) butter

FILLING

750g (1lb 10oz) cream cheese,
  softened

4 eggs

1 cup sugar

1¼ cups sour cream

3 tablespoons sugar

1 teaspoon vanilla essence

TOPPING

125g (4oz) blackberry jam

125g (4oz) blackberries

Preheat oven to 150°C (300°F).

BASE

Combine crumbs, sugar, cinnamon and butter. Press onto bottom of 23cm (9in) springform tin.

FILLING

Whip cream cheese. Add eggs one at a time, whipping after each addition. Gradually add sugar and whip. Pour over base, then bake for 45 minutes.

Whip sour cream, sugar and vanilla. Pour on top of baked cheesecake and bake for 10 more minutes. Remove and chill for at least 6 hours.

TOPPING

Heat blackberry jam and blackberries. Cool, then spread over cheesecake. Refrigerate until ready to serve, then let stand at room temperature for 10 minutes before cutting.

Lemon Cheesecake

SERVES 12

BASE

50g (1¾oz) vanilla wafers, finely
   crushed

40g (1½oz) butter, melted

3 tablespoons sugar

FILLING

340g (12oz) cream cheese

½ cup lemon juice

½ cup sugar

2 eggs, beaten

TOPPING

1 cup sour cream

zest of 2 lemons

4 tablespoons sugar

Preheat oven to 180°C (350°F).

BASE

Mix vanilla wafer crumbs, melted butter and sugar together. Press mixture firmly on bottom and sides of buttered 20cm (8in) springform tin.

FILLING

Blend cream cheese and lemon juice, add sugar and beat until smooth. Add eggs one at a time, mixing thoroughly after each addition. Pour into base, then bake for 20 minutes or until firm. Remove from oven and cool for 5 minutes only.

TOPPING

Mix sour cream, grated lemon zest and sugar, then spread over cheesecake. Bake 10 minutes longer. Cool, chill in refrigerator for at least 5 hours before serving.

   Serve with whipped cream.

Cheesecakes

Pistachio and White Mulberry Cheesecake

Serves 4

Base

60g (2oz) digestive biscuits,
  finely crushed

¼ cup sugar

30g (1oz) butter, melted

Filling

500g (17oz) cream cheese, softened

¼ cup sugar

1 tablespoon orange juice

zest of ½ orange

1 teaspoon orange blossom water

2 large eggs

Topping

zest of 1 orange

1 tablespoon orange blossom water

½ cup sugar

1 cup water

50g (1¾oz) dried white mulberries

30g (1oz) pistachios

Preheat oven to 165°C (330°F).

Base

Combine crumbs, sugar and butter. Line four 10cm (4in) springform tins with baking paper, then press mixture evenly onto bottoms of tins.

Bake for 5 minutes.

Filling

Combine cream cheese, sugar, juice, zest and orange blossom water in an electric mixer, mix on medium speed until well blended. Beat in eggs one at a time, mixing thoroughly after each addition. Divide filling evenly between each base.

Bake for 25 minutes.

Topping

Meanwhile, combine the orange zest, orange blossom water, sugar and water in a saucepan. Bring to the boil and simmer for 15 minutes. In a bowl, place the mulberries and pistachios, pour over the syrup. Cool.

Cool the cheesecakes before removing from the tins.

Decorate each cheesecake with some of the mulberries, pistachios and syrup. Serve any remaining topping on a plate.

Fruit

Hawaiian Tropics Cheesecake

SERVES 12

BASE

200g (7oz) macadamias, roasted
and chopped

FILLING

500g (17oz) cream cheese

1 cup caster (superfine) sugar

800g (1lb 12oz) ricotta

2 tablespoons plain (all-purpose)
flour

2 teaspoons ground ginger

6 large eggs

440g (15oz) canned mango slices,
drained and puréed

1 large mango, peeled and diced

¼ red pawpaw, peeled and diced

2 passionfruit

Preheat the oven to 210°C (410°F).

BASE

Line a 24cm (9½in) non-stick springform cake tin by
removing the sides and placing a large piece of baking
paper over the base. Replace the sides, resulting in a tight
false paper base. Butter the sides of the tin. Sprinkle the
macadamias over the base and set aside.

FILLING

In an electric mixer, beat the cream cheese and sugar
until the mixture is smooth. Add the ricotta, flour and
ginger and beat until just combined. Add the eggs one at a
time, beating well after each addition. Add half the mango
purée, folding through by hand to achieve a swirling effect.

Spoon into the prepared cake tin, taking care not
to disturb the placement of the crushed nuts. Sprinkle
the diced mango and pawpaw over the surface. Bake the
cheesecake for 10 minutes then reduce the heat to 160°C
(320°F). Bake for a further 50 minutes until the cake has
set and the centre is still a touch 'wobbly' (you can check
for this by gently shaking the tin).

Turn off the heat and leave the cake to cool in the oven
overnight or for at least 8 hours. Transfer the cheesecake
to the refrigerator until required. Before serving, remove
the cheesecake from the cake tin and discard the baking
paper.

To serve, mix the remaining mango purée with the
passionfruit pulp and spoon a little of this around each
slice of cheesecake. Serve with fresh cream if desired.

VARIATION

Bake the cheesecake without the fruit topping, and serve
the fruit, sliced, on the top or side of the cake.

Guava Strawberry Cheesecake

SERVES 12

BASE

125g (4oz) plain (all-purpose) flour

60g (2oz) butter

1 egg yolk

3 tablespoons lemon juice

FILLING

250g (9oz) ricotta cheese

½ cup natural yoghurt

2 eggs

2 tablespoons lemon juice

60g (2oz) sugar

250g (9oz) strawberries, sliced

100g (3½oz) guava jam

Preheat oven to 190°C (375°F).

BASE

Sift the flour into a bowl. Rub in the butter. Add the egg yolk and lemon juice, with a little cold water if required, to make a soft dough. Knead on a lightly floured surface until smooth, then press the dough evenly over the bottom of a 23cm (9in) springform tin. Rest in the refrigerator for 30 minutes.

Cover loosely with baking paper and dried beans. Bake blind for 10 minutes, remove the paper and beans and return the pastry base to the oven for 5 minutes more. Cool. Reduce the oven temperature to 180°C (350°F).

FILLING

Beat the ricotta, yoghurt, eggs, lemon juice and sugar in a bowl until smooth. Pour over the pastry base. Bake for 30 minutes or until set, then cool.

Purée 100g (3½oz) of the strawberries in a blender or food processor with the guava jam. Spread over the cheesecake. Place in the refrigerator for 1 hour. Decorate with the remaining strawberries to serve.

Blueberry Cheesecake

SERVES 12

BASE

100g (3½oz) macadamias, finely
  chopped in blender
1 cup plain (all-purpose) flour
¼ cup brown sugar, firmly packed
90g (3oz) butter, softened

FILLING

750g (1lb 10oz) cream cheese,
  softened
1½ teaspoons vanilla essence
1¼ cups sugar
4 eggs, at room temperature
1 cup sour cream

TOPPING

¾ cup warm water
¾ cup sugar
½ tablespoon gelatine
250g (9oz) fresh blueberries

Preheat oven to 200°C (400°F).

BASE

Combine base ingredients and mix well, press onto bottom
of 25cm (10in) springform tin.

Bake for 10–15 minutes. Remove from oven and allow to
cool. Reduce oven temperature to 180°C (350°F).

FILLING

Crumble cream cheese into an electric mixer. Add 1 teaspoon
of the vanilla and 1 cup of the sugar, then add eggs one at
a time, mixing well on high speed after each addition. Mix
until blended and smooth, about 4 minutes. Pour over
base.

Bake for 30 minutes until set but not completely firm.
Remove from oven, cool for 10 minutes.

Combine sour cream with remaining sugar and vanilla.
Spread over cheesecake. Bake for 5 minutes.

TOPPING

In a saucepan, place ½ cup of the water and the sugar,
bring to a boil and reduce for 10 minutes.

Meanwhile, dissolve the gelatine in the remaining water.
Add the blueberries to the sugar syrup, stir, then add the
gelatine mixture. Stir and pour over the cooled cheesecake.

Banana Brazil Nut Cheesecake

Serves 12

Base

120g (4oz) digestive biscuits, finely
    crushed

60g (2oz) Brazil nuts, ground

50g (1¾oz) butter, melted

Filling

1 vanilla pod, split in half
    lengthwise

500g (17oz) cream cheese

2 medium bananas, mashed

2 cups sour cream

1 cup sugar

3 eggs

40g (1½oz) Brazil nuts, ground

1 tablespoon banana liqueur

1 tablespoon cornflour (cornstarch)

3 tablespoons lime juice

Preheat oven to 180°C (350°F).

Base

Thoroughly mix biscuit crumbs, Brazil nuts and butter.
Spread onto bottom of 23cm (9in) springform tin. Bake
for 10 minutes.

Filling

Scrape the vanilla seeds from the pod and discard the
pod. Beat the cream cheese until soft and smooth, add
the bananas, sour cream and sugar and beat until smooth.
Add the eggs one at a time, mixing thoroughly after each
addition. Add the Brazil nuts, liqueur, cornflour, lime
juice and vanilla seeds. Mix thoroughly, then pour filling
into base.

Bake for 1 hour. Turn off the oven and leave cheesecake
in for another hour.

Serve topped with whipped cream and extra Brazil nuts.

Fruit

Boa Vista Cheesecake

SERVES 12

BASE

¾ cup instant polenta

50g (1¾oz) vanilla wafers, finely crushed

50g (1¾oz) butter, melted

FILLING

500g (17oz) cream cheese, softened

⅓ cup glucose

2 tablespoons milk

2 large eggs

½ cup macadamia nuts, toasted and chopped

¼ fresh pineapple, diced

½ fresh papaya, diced

passionfruit pulp

Preheat oven to 175°C (345°F).

BASE

Combine polenta, crumbs and butter, press onto bottom of a lined 23cm (9in) springform tin. Bake for 10 minutes.

FILLING

Combine cream cheese, glucose and milk in an electric mixer, mix on medium speed until well blended. Add eggs one at a time, mixing well after each addition. Stir in nuts, pour over base.

Bake for 45 minutes.

Loosen cake from rim, cool before removing. Chill.

Top with pineapple, papaya and passionfruit and serve.

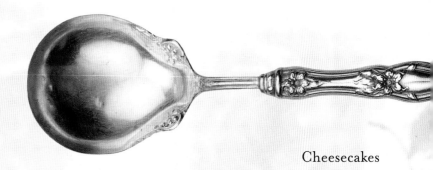

Mango Cheesecake

Serves 12

Base

90g (3oz) butter

250g (9oz) digestive biscuits, finely crushed

Filling

200g (7oz) cream cheese

50g (1¾oz) sugar

2 mangoes

1½ tablespoons gelatine

¼ cup warm water

⅔ cup thickened cream, whipped

Base

Melt the butter and stir in the biscuit crumbs. Press into the base of a lined 20cm (8in) springform tin. Chill until firm.

Filling

Place the cream cheese and sugar in a bowl and beat together.

Peel, stone and purée 1 mango, add to the cheese and sugar and mix well.

Dissolve the gelatine in the water, add to the mango mixture, then add the cream.

Mix well, spoon into the cake tin and smooth the surface. Place in refrigerator until set.

Chop the remaining mango to decorate the cheesecake and serve with extra whipped cream.

Fruit

Plum and Bitter Orange Cheesecake

Serves 12

Base

150g (5oz) gingernut biscuits

80g (2½oz) butter, melted

Filling

825g (1lb 13oz) canned plums in
   juice

500g (17oz) cream cheese, softened

½ cup sour cream

zest of ½ orange

1 tablespoon orange juice

2–3 drops Angostura bitters

3 eggs

¾ cup caster (superfine) sugar

2 tablespoons plain (all-purpose)
   flour

2 tablespoons flaked almonds

Topping

¼ cup caster (superfine) sugar

¼ cup unsweetened orange juice

zest of 1 orange

3–4 drops Angostura bitters

½ cup cream

2 teaspoons ground cinnamon

Preheat oven to 150°C (300°F).

Base

Line base of a 23cm (9in) springform tin with baking
paper.

In a food processor, process the biscuits until finely
crushed, transfer to a bowl and stir in the melted butter
until combined. Press firmly over the base of the tin,
refrigerate while preparing filling.

Filling

Drain the plums, reserving the liquid. Halve the plums
and remove the stones.

Combine the remaining filling ingredients, except the
almonds, in a large bowl. Beat with an electric mixer for
about 5 minutes or until thick and smooth.

Pour filling over the base, top with the plums and
sprinkle with almonds. Bake, uncovered, for 1 hour or
until set. Cool in the tin.

Topping

Place the reserved plum juice, sugar, juice, zest and bitters
into a small saucepan, bring to the boil, then simmer,
uncovered, until reduced by half. Allow to cool.

Combine cream and cinnamon in a bowl and whisk to
firm peaks.

Serve the cheesecake topped with the plum syrup and
cinnamon cream.

Wild Fig and Blood Orange Cheesecake

SERVES 12

BASE

180g (6oz) malt biscuits, finely
crushed

50g (1¾oz) butter, melted

FILLING

500g (17oz) cream cheese

250g (9oz) ricotta cheese

1 cup sugar

1 vanilla bean, split lengthwise

4 large eggs

TOPPING

zest of 1 blood orange

juice of 3 blood oranges

1 cup water

½ cup sugar

200g (7oz) wild figs

Preheat oven to 160°C (320°F).

BASE

Mix together the biscuit crumbs and the butter, press into
the bottom of a lined 23cm (9in) springform tin.

Bake for 10 minutes. Cool on rack while preparing
filling.

FILLING

Using an electric mixer, beat together the cream cheese,
ricotta and sugar until smooth. Scrape in seeds from
vanilla bean. Beat in eggs, one at a time, until just
blended. Pour filling over base (mixture will not fill tin).
Bake until filling is just set and puffed around edges, about
45 minutes.

TOPPING

Place all the ingredients except the figs into a saucepan,
bring to the boil, add the figs and simmer for 10 minutes.
Remove from the heat and soak for 2 hours.

Strain the figs, reserving the liquid. Return liquid to the
pan and reduce for 5 minutes to a thick syrup.

Decorate the top of the cheesecake with figs and syrup.

Fruit

Papaya Lime Cheesecake

SERVES 12

BASE

¼ cup sugar

20g (⅔ oz) butter, softened

330g (11oz) gingernut biscuits,
  finely crushed

FILLING

180g (6oz) cottage cheese

250g (9oz) cream cheese, softened

1 cup sour cream

½ cup sugar

½ cup coconut cream

¼ cup plain (all-purpose) flour

1 teaspoon coconut extract

3 eggs

TOPPING

1 cup water

1½ cups caster (superfine) sugar

3-4 fresh limes, thinly sliced

¼ papaya, cubed

Preheat oven to 175°C (345°F).

BASE

Mix together the sugar, butter and biscuit crumbs in a bowl. Press into a lined 23cm (9in) springform tin.

Bake for 12 minutes, cool on a wire rack. Lower heat to 150°C (300°F).

FILLING

Place cheeses in a food processor, process for 2 minutes or until smooth, scraping sides of processor bowl once. Add sour cream, sugar, coconut cream, flour, coconut extract and eggs, process for 20 seconds, scraping sides of processor bowl once.

Pour cheese mixture into base, bake for 1½ hours or until almost set. Turn oven off, and let cheesecake stand for 1 hour in oven with door closed. Remove cheesecake from oven, cover and chill for 1 hour.

TOPPING

Place the water and 1 cup of sugar in a pan. Bring to the boil and simmer until sugar dissolves. Add the lime slices and simmer for 10 minutes.

Meanwhile, place the remaining sugar on a tray. Remove the lime slices from the heat, strain and dry on absorbent paper. Cool slightly, then place one at a time on the tray of sugar to coat. Decorate the cheesecake with the lime slices and papaya.

Celebration

Linseed Cheesecake with Berries

SERVES 12

BASE

1 cup ground linseed

60g (2oz) digestive biscuits, finely crushed

45g (1½oz) butter, melted

FILLING

250g (9oz) cottage cheese

2 cups plain yoghurt

½ cup raw sugar

1 tablespoon plain (all-purpose) flour

1 whole egg

2 egg whites

2 teaspoons vanilla essence

125g (4oz) fresh blueberries

125g (4oz) fresh raspberries

Preheat oven to 180°C (350°F).

BASE

Mix linseed, biscuits and butter together until combined. Press into an 20cm (8in) springform tin.

Bake for 10 minutes. Cool on a rack. Reduce oven temperature to 150°C (300°F).

FILLING

In a blender or food processor, blend the cottage cheese and yoghurt for at least 1 minute. Add sugar, flour, whole egg, egg whites and vanilla. Blend until smooth.

Pour filling into base. Bake until top feels dry when lightly touched, approximately 60 minutes. Cool completely.

Decorate cheesecake with fresh blueberries and raspberries. Serve with extra berries on the side.

Cocomoco Cheesecake

Serves 12

Base

120g (4oz) digestive biscuits, finely
  crushed

3 tablespoons sugar

50g (1¾oz) butter, melted

Filling

60g (2oz) cooking chocolate

40g (1½oz) butter

500g (17oz) cream cheese, softened

1¼ cups sugar

5 large eggs

1⅓ cups flaked coconut

Topping

1 cup sour cream

2 tablespoons sugar

2 tablespoons passionfruit liqueur

1 teaspoon instant coffee

Preheat oven to 175°C (345°F).

Base

Combine crumbs, sugar and butter, press onto bottom of 23cm (9in) springform tin. Bake for 10 minutes.

Filling

Melt chocolate and butter over low heat, stirring until smooth.

Combine cream cheese and sugar in an electric mixer, mix on medium speed until well blended. Add eggs one at a time, mixing well after each addition. Blend in chocolate mixture and coconut, pour over base.

Bake for 60 minutes or until set.

Topping

Combine sour cream, sugar, liqueur and coffee, spread over cheesecake.

Reduce heat to 150°C (300°F) and bake for 5 minutes.

Loosen cake from rim of tin, cool before removing. Chill.

Baked Cherry Cheesecake

SERVES 12

BASE

60g (2oz) digestive biscuits, finely
  crushed
1 tablespoon sugar
¼ teaspoon cinnamon
¼ teaspoon nutmeg

FILLING

5 eggs
1 cup sugar
500g (17oz) cream cheese, softened
1 cup sour cream
2 tablespoons plain (all-purpose)
  flour
1 teaspoon vanilla essence

GLAZE

425g (14¾oz) canned black
  cherries
150g (5oz) black cherry jam
½ cup sugar

Preheat oven to 135°C (275°F).

BASE

Butter a 23cm (9in) springform tin and line with baking
paper.

   Combine biscuit crumbs, sugar, cinnamon and nutmeg
and sprinkle evenly over tin. Set aside.

FILLING

Separate eggs and beat yolks until lemon coloured, then
gradually add sugar. Cut cream cheese into tiny chunks,
beat until smooth, then slowly add egg yolk mixture. Beat
until smooth, then add sour cream, flour and vanilla. Beat
again until smooth. Beat egg whites until stiff but not dry.
Gently fold egg whites into cream cheese mixture. Pour
into prepared tin and bake for 70 minutes.

   Turn off heat and leave in oven for 1 hour longer
without opening oven door.

GLAZE

Drain the cherries and place ½ cup of the liquid with the
jam and sugar in a saucepan, bring to the boil and reduce
by half. Add the cherries and simmer for a further 3
minutes. Cool and pour over the cooled cheesecake.

Christmas Mincemeat Cheesecake

Serves 8–10

250g (9oz) digestive biscuits
75g (2½oz) butter
250g (9oz) cream cheese, softened
250g (9oz) cottage cheese
½ cup sugar
¼ cup cornflour (cornstarch)
4 eggs, separated
1 cup Christmas mincemeat
2 tablespoons icing sugar

Preheat oven to 200°C (400°F). Crush biscuits until coarse crumbs. Melt butter and mix into crumbs. Press over the base of a 20cm (8in) round springform tin.

Beat cream cheese, cottage cheese, sugar, cornflour and egg yolks together until smooth. Beat egg whites until stiff. Fold cheese mixture into egg whites with mincemeat.

Pour filling into the cake tin. Bake for 10 minutes then reduce heat to 180°C (350°F) and cook for a further 35–40 minutes or until set. Leave to cool in tin, then remove carefully. Serve warm or at room temperature, dusted with icing sugar.

Cheesecakes

Cheesecake Brulée

SERVES 4

BASE

60g (2oz) digestive biscuits, finely
   crushed

1/4 cup sugar

30g (1oz) butter, melted

FILLING

500g (17oz) cream cheese, softened

1/4 cup sugar

1 tablespoon lemon juice

zest of 1 small lemon

1 teaspoon vanilla essence

2 large eggs

4 tablespoons caster (superfine)
   sugar

Preheat oven to 165°C (330°F).

BASE

Combine crumbs, sugar and butter. Line four 10cm (4in) springform tins with baking paper, then press mixture evenly onto bottoms of tins.

Bake for 5 minutes.

FILLING

Combine cream cheese, sugar, juice, zest and vanilla in an electric mixer, mix on medium speed until well blended.

Beat in eggs one at a time, mixing thoroughly after each addition. Pour over base, then bake for 25 minutes. Cool before removing from tin. Chill.

Remove from refrigerator and sprinkle evenly with the caster sugar. Using a blow torch, scorch the tops of the cheesecakes and serve.

Celebration

Key Lime Cheesecake

Serves 12

Base

150g (5oz) digestive biscuits, finely
   crushed

2 tablespoons sugar

50g (1¾oz) butter, melted

Filling

570g (19oz) cream cheese, softened

¾ cup sugar

1 cup sour cream

3 tablespoons plain (all-purpose)
   flour

3 large eggs

¾ cup fresh lime juice

1 teaspoon vanilla essence

Candied Lime

1 cup water

1½ cups caster (superfine) sugar

3-4 fresh limes, thinly sliced

Preheat oven to 190°C (375°F).

Base

In a bowl, combine the crumbs and sugar, then stir in
the butter well. Pat the mixture evenly onto the bottom
and 1cm (¼in) up the sides of a buttered 25cm (10in)
springform tin. Bake the base in the centre of the oven for
8 minutes. Transfer the pan to a rack and set aside to cool.

Filling

Beat together the cream cheese and sugar with an electric
mixer until smooth. Beat in the sour cream and flour,
then add the eggs one at a time, beating well after each
addition.

   Add the lime juice and vanilla, and beat until smooth.
Pour the filling over the base. Bake for 15 minutes, reduce
the temperature to 120°C (250°F) and bake for 50–55
minutes more, or until the centre is barely set. Allow to
cool on a rack, then refrigerate, covered, overnight.

   Remove the cheesecake from the tin and transfer it to a
plate.

Candied lime

Place the water and 1 cup of the sugar in a pan. Boil until
the sugar dissolves. Add the lime slices and simmer for 10
minutes. Meanwhile place the rest of the sugar on a tray.

   Remove the limes from the heat, strain and dry on
absorbent paper. Cool slightly, then place one at a time
on the tray of sugar to coat. Place around the edge of the
cheesecake and serve.

House-Warming Cheesecakes

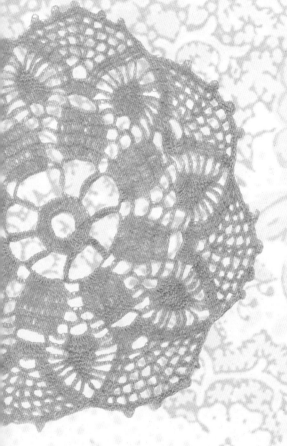

SERVES 8
250g (9oz) smooth ricotta
1 cup fruit yoghurt
½ cup puréed fruit
1 tablespoon gelatine
8 Marie biscuits

Beat ricotta and yoghurt together until smooth. Add fruit and mix well.

Dissolve gelatine in 2 tablespoons hot water, then add to ricotta mixture and mix thoroughly. Pour into 8 half-cup jelly moulds.

Lightly press a biscuit on top of each and refrigerate until set. Carefully unmould, then decorate with fresh fruit.

NOTE
Any flavoured yoghurt or purée of fruit may be used.

Cheesecakes

Winter Microwave Cheesecake

Serves 8

Base

100g (3½oz) butter

200g (7oz) plain biscuits, crushed

Filling

250g (9oz) cream cheese

250g (9oz) cottage cheese

3 eggs, lightly beaten

¾ cup sugar

1 tablespoon cornflour (cornstarch)

½ cup sour cream

grated zest of 1 lemon

3 tablespoons lemon juice

50g (1¾oz) lemon butter

Base

Melt butter in a medium-size bowl on high (100%) for 1 minute. Stir in biscuit crumbs and mix thoroughly. Press over the base and sides of a 21cm x 5cm round ovenproof dish. Refrigerate while preparing filling.

Filling

Soften cream cheese in a bowl on high (100%) for 1 minute, beat until smooth. Add cottage cheese, eggs, sugar, cornflour, sour cream, lemon zest and 1 tablespoon of the lemon juice. Beat mixture until smooth and well blended.

Pour onto biscuit crumbs and cook on medium-high (70%) for 20 minutes. Cool before removing cheesecake from dish.

Blend remaining lemon juice with lemon butter, warm on medium-low (30%) for 2 minutes and stir well. Pour over top of cheesecake. Chill thoroughly before serving.

Cheesecakes

Birthday Cheesecake

SERVES 10-12

BASE

200g (7oz) plain chocolate
    biscuits, crushed

100g (3½oz) butter, melted

FILLING

550g (19½oz) cottage cheese

¾ cup caster (superfine) sugar

½ tablespoon vanilla extract

1 tablespoon malt powder

¼ cup milk

1 cup cream

1 tablespoon gelatine

1 teaspoon cochineal (pink
    colouring)

1 teaspoon cocoa powder

2 egg whites

BASE

Combine biscuit crumbs and butter and press into the base
of a 22cm (8½in) springform tin.

FILLING

Soften cheese and beat in sugar. Add vanilla, malt powder
and milk, then fold in the cream.

Dissolve gelatine in 2 tablespoons hot water and add to
cheese mixture. Divide mixture into three and place in
separate bowls.

To one bowl add the cochineal and to another add the
cocoa. Beat egg whites until stiff and fold one-third into
each bowl. Pour pink layer onto crust base and smooth.

Gently spoon plain layer on top of the pink layer and
smooth. Finally, top with chocolate layer and smooth.

Refrigerate until firm. Decorate with whipped cream
and chocolate buttons to serve.

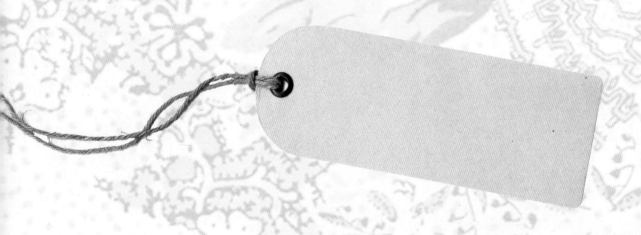

Celebration

Reunion Cheesecake

Serves 10

Base

1 sponge cake, about 2cm (³⁄₄in)
  deep and 25cm (10in) diameter
¼ cup sherry or port

Filling

250g (9oz) cream cheese
½ cup caster (superfine) sugar
2 eggs, separated
2 tablespoons lemon juice
½ cup cream
425g (14³⁄₄oz) canned sliced
  peaches, juice reserved
1 packet port wine jelly crystals

Preheat oven to 160°C (320°F).

Base

Place sponge cake on the base of a buttered 25cm (10in) springform tin and moisten with sherry or port. Beat cream cheese and sugar until smooth, then add in egg yolks, lemon juice and cream.

Filling

Beat egg whites until stiff and fold through mixture. Pour onto sponge base. Bake for 1 hour or until fairly firm. Turn off oven and leave cheesecake in it to cool.

Remove and arrange peaches on top. Mix jelly crystals with peach syrup and heat until dissolved. Cool until thick and syrupy. Pour over the cake and peaches and chill for 1–2 hours.

Holiday Cheesecake

Serves 10

Base

150g (5oz) plain sweet biscuits

30g (1oz) pecans, toasted

50g (1¾oz) margarine, melted

Filling

1½ teaspoons gelatine

zest and juice of 2 small oranges

zest and juice of 2 small lemons

350g (12oz) ricotta, well drained

¼ cup caster (superfine) sugar

1 cup sour cream

2 eggs, separated

Fruit Compote

75g (2½oz) dried figs

75g (2½oz) pitted prunes

75g (2½oz) dried apricots

75g (2½oz) dried cherries

2 tablespoons good-quality marsala

⅓ cup orange juice

zest of 1 orange

Base

Spray a 20cm (8in) springform tin with canola spray and line the base with baking paper. Process the biscuits and nuts to fine crumbs. Add the margarine and process for a few seconds to combine. Press firmly into the base of the tin. Chill for 30 minutes.

Filling

Dissolve the gelatine in a little hot water. Put the combined juices (but not the zest) in a small pot and heat gently. Add the gelatine. Remove from the heat and stir to dissolve the gelatine.

Beat the ricotta, sugar, sour cream, egg yolks and zest with an electric beater, then gradually pour in the gelatine mixture and beat slowly to combine.

Whisk the egg whites until stiff peaks form, fold 2 or 3 tablespoons of the egg whites into the ricotta mixture to lighten, then fold through the remaining egg whites, trying not to deflate the mix. Pour over the biscuit base, cover and chill for at least 3 hours. Slice into 10 portions.

Fruit Compote

To make the fruit compote, put the figs, prunes, apricots and cherries in a bowl and add the marsala, orange juice and zest. Macerate in the refrigerator overnight.

Serve with the cheesecake.

Espresso Cheesecake

Serves 12

Base

1 cup chocolate biscuit crumbs

30g (1oz) butter, melted

1 tablespoon sugar

Filling

250g (9oz) bittersweet chocolate,
   chopped

1kg (2lb 4oz) cream cheese

1 cup sugar

1 cup sour cream

2 large eggs, plus 2 egg yolks

¼ cup freshly brewed espresso coffee

1 teaspoon vanilla extract

1 tablespoon freshly ground coffee

Ganache

1 cup thickened cream

150g (5oz) bittersweet chocolate,
   chopped

1 tablespoon instant espresso coffee,
   dissolved in 2 tablespoons water

Preheat oven to 180°C (350°F).

Base

Mix together biscuits, butter and sugar in a bowl, then press into the bottom of a 22cm (8½in) springform tin. Place in refrigerator while you make the filling.

Filling

Melt chocolate in the top of a double boiler and set aside to cool. With an electric mixer, cream the cream cheese and sugar until light and fluffy, then add sour cream and mix, ensuring you scrape down the side of the bowl.

Add eggs and egg yolks until well mixed, then add espresso, vanilla, ground coffee and melted chocolate until well blended. Scrape down the sides of the bowl and blend mixture another minute to ensure it's well mixed.

Pour mixture into prepared crust, and place springform tin into a water bath. Bake for 45 minutes. Turn off oven and allow to cool slowly for at least 1 hour before removing.

Ganache

While cheesecake is cooling make ganache. In a small saucepan, bring cream to the boil, pour the chopped chocolate over and let stand for 1 minute. Stir to dissolve and then stir espresso into the chocolate mixture.

Let cool to room temperature. Pour onto top of cooled cheesecake. Refrigerate for a couple of hours to allow to set.

Engagement Cheesecake

SERVES 8-10

BASE

*150g (5oz) plain sweet biscuits,
   crushed*

75g (2½oz) butter, melted

FILLING

*450g (15oz) cottage cheese or
   cream cheese*

¾ cup caster (superfine) sugar

finely grated zest of 1 lemon

2 tablespoons lemon juice

3 eggs

1¼ cups cream

Preheat oven to 160°C (320°F).

BASE

Combine biscuits and butter together. Press firmly into base of a 20cm (8in) springform tin. Refrigerate until firm.

FILLING

Beat cheese and sugar together till smooth. Thoroughly beat in lemon zest, juice and eggs. Gently blend in cream.

Pour into prepared tin. Bake for 45 minutes. Turn off heat and leave cheesecake undisturbed in oven for a further 30 minutes. Allow to cool.

Chill in refrigerator for several hours. Decorate as desired with fresh or canned fruit and whipped cream.

Celebration

Pumpkin, Fig and Raisin Cheesecake

Serves 12

Base

1 cup semolina

2 tablespoons icing sugar

zest of ½ lemon

100g (3½oz) butter, chopped

3 teaspoons water

Filling

1 medium lime

½ cup caster (superfine) sugar

1½ cups water

2 cinnamon sticks

150g (5oz) dried figs

100g (3½oz) pumpkin, mashed and cooled

180g (6oz) kashta cheese

2 teaspoons cornflour (cornstarch)

3 egg yolks

¾ cup thickened cream

¼ cup raisins

zest of ½ lemon

1 tablespoon dark rum

Preheat oven to 180°C (350°F).

Base

Grease a 23cm (9in) springform tin. Mix semolina, sugar and lemon zest, rub in butter until mixture resembles fine breadcrumbs. Add enough water to make ingredients come together.

Press evenly into prepared tin. Bake for 15 minutes or until lightly browned. Allow to cool.

Filling

Remove zest from lime, combine with 1½ tablespoons of the sugar, the water and cinnamon in a medium saucepan, stir over heat until sugar is dissolved. Bring to the boil, add figs and simmer uncovered for 5 minutes. Remove from heat, stand for 3 hours.

Preheat oven to 180°C (350°F). Remove figs from syrup, pat dry and finely chop. Whisk pumpkin, cheese, cornflour, remaining sugar and egg yolks in a bowl until combined. Add chopped figs, cream, raisins, lemon zest and rum, mix well.

Pour filling over base, bake for 50 minutes or until the centre of the cheesecake is almost set. Turn oven off, cool cheesecake in oven with door ajar.

Note

Kashta is a heavy cream style of fresh cheese. Ask for it in local Lebanese and Middle Eastern supermarkets.

Spring Ice Cream Cheesecake

SERVES 8–10

BASE

2 cups plain sweet biscuit crumbs

170g (6oz) butter, melted

FILLING

375g (13oz) cream cheese, softened

¾ cup caster (superfine) sugar

200g (7oz) fresh or frozen berries

4 cups vanilla ice cream

BASE

Combine biscuit crumbs and butter in a bowl and mix well. Press mixture over base and sides of a 20cm (8in) springform tin and refrigerate until firm.

FILLING

Beat cheese and sugar together in a bowl until the mixture is smooth. Blend or process berries until smooth, then add to the cheese mixture.

Chop up the ice cream, add to the cheese mixture and beat until smooth.

Pour filling into crust and freeze for several hours or until firm. Decorate with whipped cream and fresh berries.

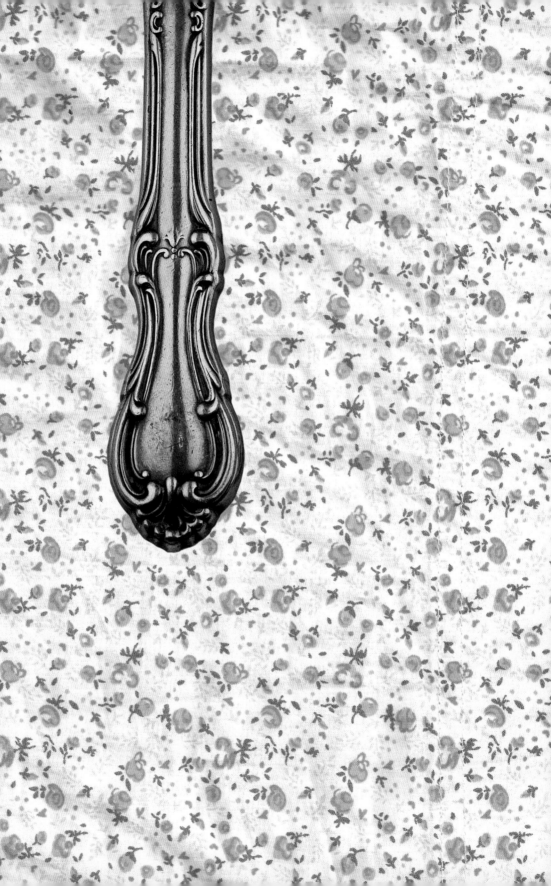

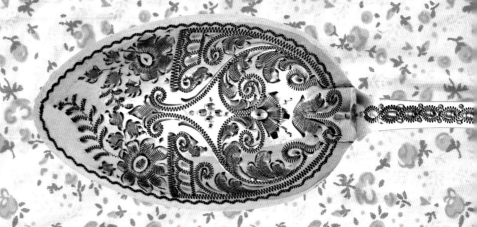

Mini

Calypso Cheesecake

Serves 4

Base

¾ *cup ground almonds*

20g (⅔oz) *butter, melted*

Filling

1½ *tablespoons gelatine*

¼ *cup water*

450g (15oz) *cream cheese*

¾ *cup milk*

¾ *cup sugar*

2 *tablespoons rum*

Topping

¼ *cup water*

½ *cup sugar*

2 *tablespoons rum*

¼ *pineapple, cut into small pieces*

toasted shredded coconut

BASE

Stir together almonds and butter in a small bowl.

Line four 10cm (4in) springform tins with baking paper, then press mixture evenly onto bottoms of tins.

FILLING

Soften gelatine in water in a small saucepan, stir over low heat until dissolved. Beat cream cheese, milk, sugar and rum in an electric mixer until well blended. Stir in the gelatine and mix well. Pour into the springform tins, refrigerate for 3 hours or overnight.

TOPPING

Combine the water, sugar and rum in a saucepan, bring to the boil then simmer for 15 minutes. Add the pineapple pieces to the syrup and cool.

Divide topping evenly between cheesecakes, then top with coconut.

Raspberry Cheesecake

SERVES 4

BASE

*60g (2oz) digestive biscuits,
    finely crushed*

30g (1oz) butter, melted

¼ cup sugar

FILLING

500g (17oz) cream cheese, softened

1 tablespoon lemon juice

1 teaspoon vanilla essence

¼ cup sugar

2 large eggs

125g (4oz) fresh raspberries

Preheat oven to 165°C (330°F).

BASE

Combine crumbs, butter and sugar. Line four 10cm (4in) springform tins with baking paper, then press mixture evenly onto bottoms of tins.

Bake for 5 minutes.

FILLING

Combine cream cheese, juice, vanilla and sugar in an electric mixer, mix on medium speed until well combined. Add the eggs one at a time, mixing well after each addition. Gently fold through ¾ of the raspberries. Divide filling evenly between each base. Top cheesecakes with the remaining raspberries.

Bake for 25 minutes. Cool before removing from tins.

Mini

Plum Cheesecakes with Passionfruit Sauce

SERVES 4

100g (3½oz) cream cheese

¼ cup condensed milk

1 egg yolk

1 large sheet puff pastry

2 plums, roughly chopped

170g (6oz) canned passionfruit pulp

Preheat oven to 200°C (400°F).

In a food processor, combine cream cheese, condensed milk and egg yolk, beat until thick and creamy.

Using a pastry cutter 12cm in diameter, cut 4 rounds out of the pastry. Cut five 2cm-long incisions into the sides of the pastry at regular intervals. Place pastry rounds into large muffin tin moulds, making sure that the pastry slightly overlaps where the incisions have been made.

Add quarter of the plums to each pastry case, then top each with a quarter of the cheese mixture.

Cook for 6–8 minutes or until cheesecakes are set and lightly browned. Allow to cool, then serve with passionfruit pulp.

Cheesecakes

Apple Cream Cheesecake

SERVES 8
8 coconut biscuits
250g (9oz) cream cheese
3 eggs
¾ cup sugar
1 cup cream
415g (14 ½oz) canned apples
grated zest of 1 lemon
2 tablespoons gelatine
½ cup sweet white wine

Place a biscuit in the base of eight paper-lined half-cup capacity ramekins.

Soften cream cheese and beat with eggs and sugar until smooth. Whip cream until soft peaks form. Fold into cream cheese mixture with apple and lemon zest.

Soften gelatine in wine. Stand over hot water until gelatine dissolves. Mix into cream cheese mixture. Divide mixture evenly among ramekins. Refrigerate until set.

Run a knife around the edge of each ramekin. Turn onto serving plates. Serve garnished with apple slices and toasted coconut.

Mini

Passionfruit and Lychee Cheesecake

Serves 4

Base

60g (2oz) digestive biscuits, finely
   crushed

¼ cup sugar

30g (1oz) butter, melted

Filling

500g (17oz) cream cheese, softened

¼ cup passionfruit pulp, strained

¼ cup sugar

2 large eggs

8 lychees

Preheat oven to 165°C (330°F).

Base

Combine crumbs, sugar and butter. Line four 10cm (4in)
springform tins with baking paper, then press mixture
evenly onto bottoms of tins.

Bake for 5 minutes.

Filling

Combine cream cheese, pulp and sugar in an electric
mixer, mix on medium speed until well blended. Beat in
eggs one at a time, mixing thoroughly after each addition.
Divide filling evenly between bases.

Bake for 25 minutes.

Cool the cheesecakes before removing from the tins.

Decorate with extra pulp and lychees.

Cheesecakes

Continental Nougat

SERVES 4

BASE

¾ *cup ground almonds*

20g *(⅔oz) butter, melted*

FILLING

1½ *tablespoons gelatine*

¼ *cup water*

450g *(15oz) cream cheese*

¾ *cup milk*

¾ *cup sugar*

2 *teaspoons almond essence*

100g *(3½oz) nougat, cut into small*
   pieces

BASE

Stir together almonds and butter in a small bowl.

Line four 10cm (4in) springform tins with baking paper, then press mixture evenly onto bottoms of tins.

FILLING

Soften gelatine in water in a small saucepan, stir over low heat until dissolved. Beat cream cheese, milk, sugar and almond essence with an electric mixer until well blended. Stir in the gelatine.

Divide filling evenly between tins, place in refrigerator for 3 hours or overnight.

Top each cheesecake with nougat pieces and serve.

Mini

Basil and Sun-Dried Tomato Cheesecakes

Serves 6

30g (1oz) butter, melted

1 cup pistachio kernels, finely chopped

250g (9oz) cream cheese

250g (9oz) ricotta

½ cup sour cream

2 large eggs

½ teaspoon salt

¼ teaspoon freshly ground black pepper

2 teaspoons mild paprika

½ bunch chives, chopped

12 sun-dried tomatoes in oil, drained and finely chopped

1 cup tightly packed basil leaves, finely sliced

Preheat the oven to 190°C (375°F).

Generously grease a large muffin tin with six indentations, or alternatively 6 large soufflé dishes, with the butter. Sprinkle the chopped nuts over the inside of each muffin indentation or soufflé dish so that they are entirely coated.

In a large mixing bowl, beat the cream cheese and ricotta together until well mixed. Add the sour cream, eggs, salt and pepper to taste, and the paprika, and beat well until smooth. Add the chives and set aside.

Add tomatoes and basil to the cheese mixture and stir thoroughly.

Spoon the mixture into the prepared muffin tin or soufflé dishes and bake for 15 minutes. Reduce the heat to 140°C (285°F) and bake for a further 10 minutes. Remove from the oven and set aside to cool.

Turn the little cheesecakes out of the tins and serve warm or cold garnished with extra sun-dried tomatoes, basil and sour cream or with a side salad.

NOTE

To serve warm, it is better to bake the cheesecakes ahead and cool, then reheat gently in the microwave.

Fruits of the Forest Cheesecake

SERVES 4

BASE

60g (2oz) digestive biscuits, finely
    crushed

30g (1oz) butter, melted

¼ cup sugar

FILLING

500g (17oz) cream cheese, softened

1 tablespoon lemon juice

1 teaspoon vanilla essence

¼ cup sugar

2 large eggs

TOPPING

140g (5oz) frozen mixed berries

½ cup strawberry jam

¼ cup sugar

Preheat oven to 165°C (330°F).

BASE

Combine crumbs, butter and sugar. Line four 10cm (4in) springform tins with baking paper, then press mixture evenly onto bottoms of tins.

Bake for 5 minutes.

FILLING

Combine cream cheese, juice, vanilla and sugar in an electric mixer, mix on medium speed until well combined. Add the eggs one at a time, mixing well after each addition. Pour filling over the base.

Bake for 25 minutes. Cool before removing from tins.

TOPPING

Meanwhile, in a small saucepan over a low heat combine the berries, jam and sugar. Simmer gently for 10 minutes, stirring occasionally. Remove from the heat and cool.

Once both the cheesecakes and the berries are cool, spoon the berry topping over each cheesecakes and serve immediately.

Mini

Rocky Road Cheesecake

Serves 4

Base

¾ *cup ground almonds*

20g (⅔oz) *butter, melted*

Filling

1½ *tablespoons gelatine*

¼ *cup water*

450g (15oz) *cream cheese*

¾ *cup milk*

¾ *cup sugar*

¼ *teaspoon vanilla essence*

200g (7oz) *rocky road, chopped
   into small pieces*

Base

Stir together almonds and butter in a small bowl.

Line four 10cm (4in) springform tins with baking paper, then press mixture evenly onto bottoms of tins.

Filling

Soften gelatine in water in a small saucepan, stir over low heat until dissolved. Beat cream cheese, milk, sugar and vanilla essence with an electric mixer until well blended. Stir in half the rocky road then the gelatine. Divide filling evenly between tins, place in refrigerator for 3 hours or overnight.

Decorate with extra rocky road and serve.

Cheesecakes

Sultana and Bourbon Cheesecake

SERVES 4

BASE

60g (2oz) digestive biscuits, finely crushed

30g (1oz) butter, melted

¼ cup sugar

FILLING

1½ cups raisins

¼ cup Bourbon

500g (17oz) cream cheese, softened

¼ cup sugar

1 tablespoon lemon juice

zest of ½ lemon

2 large eggs

Soak the raisins in the Bourbon for at least 2 hours.

Preheat oven to 165°C (330°F).

BASE

Combine crumbs, butter and sugar. Line four 10cm (4in) springform tins with baking paper, then press mixture evenly onto bottoms of tins. Bake for 5 minutes.

FILLING

Combine cream cheese, sugar, juice and zest in an electric mixer, mix on medium speed until well blended. Add eggs one at a time, mixing thoroughly between additions. Chop 1 cup of the soaked raisins roughly and add to the filling, then divide filling evenly between tins.

Bake for 25 minutes. Cool before removing from tins, then chill.

Let stand at room temperature for minimum of 40 minutes. Decorate with the remaining raisins and serve with whipped cream.

Mini

Mini Passionfruit Cheesecake

SERVES 4

BASE

60g (2oz) digestive biscuits, finely crushed

30g (1oz) butter, melted

¼ cup sugar

FILLING

500g (17oz) cream cheese, softened

¼ cup passionfruit pulp, strained

1 teaspoon vanilla essence

¼ cup sugar

2 large eggs

4 fresh passionfruit

Preheat oven to 165°C (330°F).

BASE

Combine crumbs, butter and sugar. Line four 10cm (4in) springform tins with baking paper, then press mixture evenly onto bottoms of tins.

Bake for 5 minutes.

FILLING

Combine cream cheese, passionfruit pulp, vanilla and sugar in an electric mixer, mix on medium speed until well combined. Add the eggs one at a time, mixing well after each addition. Divide filling evenly between the bases.

Bake for 25 minutes. Cool before removing from tins.

Decorate with fresh passionfruit and serve.

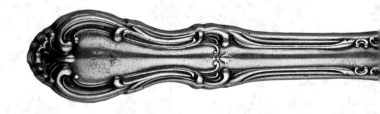

Cheesecake Cookies

SERVES 12

BASE

70g (2 ½ oz) butter, softened

⅓ cup brown sugar, packed

1 cup plain (all-purpose) flour

FILLING

½ cup sugar

250g (9oz) cream cheese, softened

1 egg

2 tablespoons milk

1 tablespoon lemon juice

½ teaspoon vanilla

Preheat oven to 180°C (350°F).

BASE

In a medium bowl, blend the butter, brown sugar and flour with a fork until mixture resembles coarse crumbs.

Put 1 cup of the mixture aside for topping. Press remaining mixture into a 20 x 20 x 5cm (8 x 8 x 2in) baking dish, bake for 15 minutes. Remove from oven and allow to cool.

FILLING

In another bowl combine sugar and cream cheese, mixing until smooth. Thoroughly beat in egg, milk, lemon juice and vanilla. Spread over the baked base and sprinkle with remaining brown sugar mixture. Bake for 25 minutes. Cool, then chill for at least 1 hour. Cut into 12 squares.

Mini

Mini Fruit Cheesecakes

Serves 4

Base

150g (5oz) digestive biscuits,
    crushed
30g (1oz) butter, melted
¼ cup sugar

Filling

1½ tablespoons gelatine
500g (17oz) cream cheese
¾ cup milk
1 teaspoon vanilla extract
¾ cup caster (superfine) sugar

Topping

400g (14oz) canned sliced peaches
20 fresh blueberries

Base

Combine biscuits, butter and sugar together. Line four 10cm (4in) springform tins with baking paper, then press mixture firmly and evenly into base of pans. Refrigerate until firm.

Filling

Soften gelatine in ¼ cup water in a small saucepan, stir over low heat until dissolved.

Beat cream cheese, milk, vanilla and sugar with an electric mixer, mix on medium until well combined. Pour into prepared tins.

Leave cheesecake undisturbed in the refrigerator for 3 hours or overnight.

Decorate with sliced peaches with blueberries piled on top.

Mini Currant and Lemon Cheesecake

SERVES 4

BASE

60g (2oz) digestive biscuits, finely
 crushed
30g (1oz) butter, melted
¼ cup sugar

FILLING

500g (17oz) cream cheese, softened
2 tablespoons lemon juice
zest of 2 lemons
¼ cup sugar
2 large eggs
½ cup currants

TOPPING

finely grated zest of 2 lemons
1 cup caster (superfine) sugar

Preheat oven to 165°C (330°F).

BASE

Combine crumbs, butter and sugar. Line four 10cm (4in) springform tins with baking paper, then press mixture evenly onto bottoms of tins.

Bake for 5 minutes.

FILLING

Combine cream cheese, juice, zest and sugar in an electric mixer, mix on medium speed until well combined. Add the eggs one at a time, mixing well after each addition. Stir through the currants, then pour filling over the base.

Bake for 25 minutes.

TOPPING

Meanwhile, place the lemon zest in a small saucepan and cover with water. Bring to the boil and simmer for 5 minutes. Drain and rinse the zest. In a small saucepan, combine half the sugar with ½ cup water and bring to the boil, add the zest and simmer for 10 minutes. Meanwhile, place the remaining sugar on a tray. Remove zest from the sugar syrup, strain and dry on absorbent paper. Cool slightly, then roll in the tray of sugar until well coated.

Once cooled, remove the cheesecakes from the tins, dust with icing sugar and top with the candied lemon zest.

Chocolate and Orange Jaffa

Serves 4

Base

60g (2oz) digestive biscuits, finely
    crushed

30g (1oz) butter, melted

Filling

¼ cup sugar

1½ cups sour cream

1 cup sugar

2 eggs

1 teaspoon vanilla essence

500g (17oz) cream cheese, broken
    into small pieces

40g (1½oz) butter, melted

Preheat oven to 165°C (330°F).

Base

Combine the crumbs, butter and sugar. Line four 10cm
(4in) springform tins with baking paper, then press
mixture evenly onto bottoms of tins.

Bake for 5 minutes.

Filling

Combine cream cheese, juice, zest and sugar in an electric
mixer, mix on medium speed until well combined. Add
eggs one at a time. Stir through the chocolate. Divide
filling evenly between tins.

Bake for 25 minutes. Cool before removing from tins.

Cheesecakes

Notes

Cheesecakes

Notes

Cheesecakes

Notes

Notes

Cheesecakes

Index

191

A Note on Measurements

¼ teaspoon	1.25ml
½ teaspoon	2.5ml
1 teaspoon	5g/5ml
1 tablespoon	15g/15ml

Liquid measures: 1 cup = 250ml (9fl oz)

Solid measures (vary, depending on substance)

eg: caster (superfine) sugar: 1 cup = 220g (7oz)

plain (all-purpose) flour: 1cup = 150g (4¾oz)

First published in 2012 by

New Holland Publishers

London • Sydney • Cape Town • Auckland

www.newhollandpublishers.com

Garfield House 86–88 Edgware Road London W2 2EA United Kingdom

1/66 Gibbes Street Chatswood NSW 2067 Australia

Wembley Square First Floor Solan Road Gardens Cape Town 8001 South Africa

218 Lake Road Northcote Auckland New Zealand

A catalogue record of this book is available at the British Library and the National Library of Australia

ISBN: 9781742573373

Publisher: Fiona Schultz

Publishing director: Lliane Clarke

Design: Tracy Loughlin

Production director: Olga Dementiev

Printer: Toppan Leefung Printing Limited

10 9 8 7 6 5 4 3 2 1

Follow New Holland Publishers on

Facebook: www.facebook.com/NewHollandPublishers

UK £14.99
US $19.99